Every Step a Prayer

Every Step a Prayer:
The Lives of Black Mothers Raising Black Sons

Dr. Michelle Wright-Carter

Warrior Princess Nation, LLC

Copyright ©2025 by Dr. Michelle Wright-Carter

All rights reserved. No part of this book may be reproduced in any manner whatsoever without the written permission of the author or publisher except in the case of brief quotations embodied in critical articles and reviews.

Warrior Publishing, a division of
Warrior Princess Nation, LLC
6935 Aliante Pkwy Ste 104 #423
North Las Vegas, NV 89084
for information email info@warriorprincessnation.com

First Printing, 2025

Dissertation presented to the Faculty of the
California School of Professional Psychology
Alliant International University
Sacramento
In fulfillment of the requirements for the degree of
Doctor of Psychology
by
Michelle Wright, M.A.   2024

Approved by:
Dr. Tatiana Glebova, Ph.D., Chairperson
Dr. Gita Seshadri, Ph.D.
Dr. Franchesca Fontus, Ph.D.

Table of Contents

Dedication	9
Acknowledgments	10
Abstract	12
List of Tables	13
Chapter I Introduction	14
Statement of the Problem	18
Purpose and Significance of the Study	19
Theoretical Framework	20
Definition of Terms	22
Research Question	23
Chapter II Literature Review	25
History of Racism	25
Modern Manifestation of Racism	28
Fears of Parenting within a Racist Society	30
History of Critical Race Theory (CRT)	32
Definition of CRT	32
How CRT Explains Racism	32
CRT and Racism - Implications on the Treatment of Young Black Men	33
History of Police Brutality Towards Black Americans	35
Racial Disparities in Police Brutality	38
Black Mothers Experience Racism and Police Brutality	39
Black Mothers' Impact of Possibly Losing Their Son to Police Brutality	40
Mothers' Grief	42
Black Motherhood	43
Chapter III Methods	46
Phenomenological Approach	46
Transcendental Phenomenology	47
Participants	49
Protection of Participants	49
Sampling Procedures	51
Data Collection Methods	52
Demographic Questionnaire	52

Face-to-Face Video-Recorded Interview	52
Interview Procedures	53
Data Analysis Plan	53
Trustworthiness	55
Credibility	56
Transferability	57
Dependability	58
Confirmability	58
Chapter IV Results	60
Findings	61
Data Analysis	61
Step 1: Horizontalization	62
Step 2: Data Reduction and Elimination	62
Step 3: Identification of Invariant Constituents	63
Step 4: Thematizing Invariant Constituents	63
Step 5: Validating Invariant Constituent Themes	65
Step 6: Developing Textural Descriptions	65
Step 7: Developing Structural Descriptions	66
Step 8: Developing Composite Textural-Structural Descriptions	66
Themes	68
Theme 1: Benefits of Raising a Black Male Child Included Passing on Values and Serving as a Role Model and Protector	68
Theme 2: Racism Had Negative Impacts on the Experience of Raising a Black Male Child	72
Theme 3: Black Mothers Empower Their Black Male Children Against the Impacts of Racism	77
Theme 4: Law Enforcement Perceived as a Threat to Black Male Children	82
Theme 5: Black Mothers Navigated the Fear of Losing Their Sons Through Educating Their Sons and Through Reliance on Faith	89
Summary	93
Chapter V Discussion	94
Self as a Researcher	97

Summary of the Findings	100
Interpretation of the Findings	101
Theme 1: Benefits of Raising a Black Male Child Included Passing on Values and Serving as a Role Model and Protector	101
Theme 2: Racism Had Negative Impacts on the Experience of Raising a Black Male Child	102
Theme 3: Black mothers empower their Black male children against the impacts of racism	103
Theme 4: Law Enforcement is Perceived as a Threat to Black Male Children	105
Theme 5: Black Mothers Navigated the Fear of Losing Their Sons Through Educating Their Sons and Through Reliance on Faith	107
Implications of the Study	108
Limitations	110
Recommendations for Future Research	111
Conclusion	113
References	115
APPENDIX A Email to Participants	122
APPENDIX B Informed Consent Agreement	124
APPENDIX C Demographic Information	131
APPENDIX D Interview Questions	134
APPENDIX E Recruitment Flyer	137
Author Bio	139

Dedication

I dedicate this dissertation to, most importantly, God. Without the guidance of the Trinity, God the Father, God the Son, and God the Holy Spirit, this dissertation would have never come to fruition. Philippians 4:13 is one of my favorite Scriptures. I can do all things through Christ, who gives me strength. To my parents, Robert and Doris Wright, who gave me life and instilled in me at an early age that this world has room for me and that I can become anything I desire to be. To my beautiful children Steven, Ronkiesha, Demario, Deandre, and my amazing grandchildren, who are the loves of my life, my children give me purpose. My grandchildren gave me the chance to instill in them the wisdom and courage my grandmother instilled in me. To my grandson, baby Demario, who passed away at a young age. My grandmother, Carrie Lee Richards, aka "granny," was the matriarch of our family. She was a beautiful, strong Black woman, and she significantly influenced my upbringing. She provided values, morals, love, respect, and a great sense of security in an unsafe world for African Americans. To my husband, one of the loves of my life Edward Carter, and my best friend, my brother Gerald Wayne Jonhson, who was an incredible support system. Willie Graham, my pastor of 26 years, who gave me spiritual guidance throughout this process, and finally, my baby brother Robert Wright Jr., whose life was senselessly and tragically taken away. Everyone played a pivotal role in my life and were my biggest supporters throughout this process, some in spirit because they are no longer physically here. In addition, they all were the inspiration, motivation, and encouragement that propelled me to continue to move forward in completing this enormous task God put before me. Thank you all for assisting and being there when things were extremely difficult for me; thank you for loving me unconditionally through it all.

Acknowledgments

I want to express my gratitude to all those who aided and supported me during my dissertation journey. It is a great privilege to acknowledge their contributions. Doctoral students are strongly recommended to carefully consider their choice of chairperson. Among the exceptional faculty members, I decided early in my program to choose Dr. Tatiana Glebova as my chair. I was initially excited by her enthusiasm for my dissertation topic. At that moment, I realized that we would be a great match. We met on a weekly basis and, on occasion, twice a week to bring this sensitive but meaningful body of work to fruition. Dr. Glebova utilized her extensive expertise, knowledge, and skills to provide me with unwavering support throughout this process, offering valuable counsel, feedback, clarity, and understanding. I cannot emphasize enough the enormous amount of help she provided during the process of finalizing my dissertation. I am eternally appreciative of her support. I want to acknowledge my dissertation committee members. I consider myself extremely blessed to have had an exceptional committee composed of Dr. Branson Boykins and Dr. Gita Seshadri. They always made themselves accessible, and it was reassuring to know that I could seek their assistance if I encountered difficulties or had questions.

Additionally, I would like to extend my gratitude to Dr. Franchesca Fontus for her gracious participation as a committee member during the absence of Dr. Boykin. Acknowledging the ten exceptional African American mothers' significant contributions to this study is an honor. Being a part of my participants' lived experience was an extraordinary opportunity. Words cannot express how deeply grateful and appreciative I am for their willingness to share their heart, thoughts, emotions, feelings, and, most importantly, their voice. Listening to each of their experiences has profoundly impacted me as a Black mother. Thank you for giving this opportunity to other mothers who may read this dissertation. I want to acknowledge my church family, Christian Body Life Fellowship, for their countless prayers. I also want to thank Ashely Moore, Ryan McMurray, Dr. Laura Pedersen, Dr. Willie Jamal Graham, Ashley Harrinauth, Briana Schiff, Mother Barbara Cotton, and my four bonus children Rico, Shaveda, Elece, Edward Jr. Each of them has played a significant role in assisting me with my dissertation, including providing valuable feedback, proofreading, and editing, offering encouragement and support, and strengthening me throughout my most difficult moments. I firmly believe God divinely selected every one of these extraordinary individuals I mentioned in my acknowledgments to assist me in successfully finishing my dissertation and ultimately achieving my doctoral degree. Thank you.

Abstract

The prevalence of police violence against the African American community has been well-documented, and there are many examples of unarmed Black men fatally shot by law enforcement. Police brutality has several deleterious effects on African American communities; however, the effects on Black mothers are overlooked. This study examined and amplified voices and collective experiences of how Black mothers navigate their fears of the possibility of losing their sons when encountering law enforcement in an inherently discriminatory world. The study employed Critical Race Theory as a theoretical framework and focused on counter-storytelling as a means of challenging the dominant cultural paradigm. Interviews were conducted with ten self-identified African American mothers over the age of eighteen with at least one Black male child. Analysis of the interview sessions produced several emergent themes. Benefits described by participants included the opportunity to pass on personal values and serve as a role model for one's children. Participants stated that law enforcement is perceived as a threat, and racism had a negative effect on raising a Black male child. However, participants mitigated fears of losing a child to police violence by educating their sons while relying on faith. Results illuminated the structural nature of racism in the U.S. and the ways existing social institutions perpetuate racial privilege for the dominant, White-centered culture. Given an inequitable social and cultural playing field, the implications for practitioners' trend towards the use of culturally and socially inclusive strategies for clients, particularly for African Americans and other historically marginalized populations.

List of Tables

Table 1. Demographic Information
Table 2. Invariant Constituent Themes (Initial Codes)
Table 3. Invariant Constituent Themes (Initial Codes) Designated as Textural Descriptions
Table 4. Invariant Constituent Themes (Initial Codes) Designated as Structural Descriptions
Table 5. Grouping of Textural and Structural Descriptions into Final Composite Themes

Chapter I

Introduction

Historically, the presence of police in the Black community in the United States (U.S.) has elicited fear and mistrust, and this sentiment persists in the 21st century. This overarching attitude towards law enforcement stems from years of policing in slaveholding states, which had roots in slave patrols, squadrons made up of White volunteers empowered to use vigilante tactics to enforce laws related to slavery (Hassett-Walker, 2020). In the U.S., the potential for unjust policing to foster fear is enormous. These negative feelings still resonate today among Black Americans (Harris & Amutah-Onukagha, 2019). The distinct loss of Black life surrounding police encounters has increased international and domestic awareness regarding the influence of race on the U.S. Criminal Justice System, especially in reference to policing (Smith, Lee, & Robinson, 2019). Police killings are "A case where a person dies as a result of being chased, beaten, arrested, restrained, shot, pepper-sprayed, tasered, or otherwise harmed by police officers, whether on-duty or off-duty, intentional or accidental" (DeAngelis, 2021). According to Harris and Amutah-Onukagha (2019), the heightened awareness surrounding police violence has produced significant knowledge regarding the effects of police interactions on Black families.

The role of Black parents is crucial in equipping their children for the world in which they live, particularly in a society where interactions with law enforcement are common (Cabrera et al., 2016). Black mothers, who are frequently assigned the role of primary caregivers, face the challenge of balancing their parental responsibilities with the demands of daily living, all while ensuring that their children are prepared to navigate a society that perpetuates racism (Elliot et al., 2015; Woods & Kurtz-Costes, 2007). The distinct socialization process experienced by Black mothers and their children encompasses acquiring knowledge regarding societal norms while also taking into consideration the presence of both implicit and explicit racism. Harris and Amutah-Onukagha (2019) organized a focus group of six Black mothers with sons aged between 11 and 33 years. The findings uncovered the strategies and guidelines that Black mothers who participated in the study imparted to their boys to equip them for possible interaction with law enforcement and improve their safety. Some of these strategies and instructions included telling their sons the harsh realities of being Black, how to regulate their behavior, and reiterating to their sons that their family and community support them, as well as attempting to reframe the negative thoughts and feelings that the Black community has toward police.

    Little is known about how Black mothers protect their sons in a society where racism, discrimination, and police brutality produce fear within Black Americans. Black mothers have a profound and pervasive fear for their children, particularly their sons, who are at a higher risk of being killed in routine daily activities than children of other races. This fear is by no means unjustified, given the fact that police brutality is a leading cause of death among young Black men in the U.S. (Edwards et al., 2019). Furthermore, Black males are twice as likely to be killed by law enforcement officers before reaching the age of 21 compared to their White counterparts. According to Harris and Amutah-Onukagha (2019), the prevalence of police violence among young Black males increases their vulnerability to fatality or physical harm in the context of police contact. Black mothers often express fears about the burden placed on them to ensure the safety of their children, particularly considering the additional challenges arising from racial discrimination and mistreatment. As a result, a mother's worry, fear, and stress intensify negatively affecting Black families overall. Edwards et al. (2019) assert that Black men are at the most significant risk of experiencing fatal encounters with law enforcement, with a 1 in 1,000 probability of being killed by police over their lifetime. The risk reaches its highest point between the ages of 20 and 35. Overall, for young men of color, the utilization of violent force by the police is one of the primary factors contributing to death. Research has also indicated that Black boys have a higher likelihood of receiving adult sentences compared to their White counterparts.

Additionally, police officers tend to see Black youth as older and more culpable than White adolescents (Carbado & Rock, 2016). For example, the police officer who fatally shot Tamir Rice, a 12-year-old African American adolescent, had a perception of him as being older than his actual age (Fitzimmons, 2014; Staggers-Hakim, 2016). The highly publicized police killings of Black boys and men have unveiled a life-course incidence of homicide deaths among Black males resulting from police violence throughout the country (Smith et al., 2019).

Examining U.S. history offers the opportunity to reflect on the country's past involving racial inequality. Furthermore, exploring the past and present connections between race and the U.S. justice system helps us better understand the current climate surrounding nationwide debates about racial discrimination, police brutality, White supremacy, White privilege, and systemic racism (Bundles, 2015). Racism has been deeply ingrained in the nation's policies, spaces, economic structures, and social norms since its conception (Lavalley & Johnson, 2020). Racism has permeated many experiences individuals encounter living in the U.S. Violence against Black males at the hands of authority figures is ingrained within U.S. society and continues to influence policing culture today (Lavalley & Johnson, 2020).

Furthermore, a multitude of distinct occurrences of police brutality in the U.S. have been brought to light because of heightened media coverage. The issue of lethal force used by law enforcement, especially against minority groups, has gained significant public attention in recent years. This increased scrutiny is a result of several well-known cases involving the killings of unarmed Black men and teenagers by the police (DeGue et al., 2016). The widespread protests sparked by these cases have given rise to civil unrest and the emergence of the Black Lives Matter movement. For example, George Floyd was a 46-year-old Black man who died after a White Minneapolis police officer kneeled on his neck for over nine minutes in May of 2020. In George Floyd's final moments of life, he called out for his mother. The final words made by Floyd have served as a unifying force for mothers who have experienced the loss of their children due to instances of police brutality throughout the years (Gold, 2020). Kadiatou Diallo is the mother of Amadou Diallo, a Black man who was fatally shot 41 times by police in 1999. This occurred after Mr. Diallo reached into his pocket while police had him surrounded, and, as in so many other cases, it was assumed he was reaching for a weapon. After examining Mr. Diallo's body, he was found to be holding his wallet, which held his identification. (Ghebremedhin et al., 2020).

Similarly, Valerie Bell endured profound sorrow following the police shooting of her son, Sean Bell, a few hours prior to his wedding in 2006. Another mother, Constance Malcolm, experienced every parent's worst nightmare after police followed Ramarley Graham, her 17-year-old son, into his residence in 2012 and fatally shot him in the presence of his six-year-old brother. The police alleged to have observed a firearm on the unarmed Black teenager (Khushbu, 2020). Unfortunately, these are only a few names and a few mothers, out of many more, whose lives have been forever altered due to these racially charged acts of violence and discrimination. However, despite the frequency of police brutality within Black communities, few studies have examined how these horrific losses impact Black mothers and exacerbate their fear of losing their sons to police violence.

Statement of the Problem

In recent years, a series of highly publicized killings of unarmed Black males at the hands of police officers in the U.S. have evoked national outrage (Hall & Perry, 2016). However, in the wake of these unexpected killings, one population has been overlooked: Black mothers. The lack of acknowledgment and thought toward these mothers who fear losing their sons to police brutality is devastating and should not be disregarded. Although it is certainly true that Black fathers also experience intense feelings of concern for their sons, this study focused on Black mothers for several reasons. For example, Black mothers often take on the responsibility of raising and protecting their sons and maneuvering through their racially charged environment. Though motherhood is different for every mother, a Black mother, regardless of the context of their cultural and social background, educational attainment, and socioeconomic status, instinctively understands what it means to give birth and raise a Black male child (Warner, 2020). Black mothers go through traumatizing experiences that change their lives forever in a society that historically does not value or consider the struggle of racism and its effects on Black families (Taylor, 2019). The problem is that Black mothers face a set of unique challenges in that there is an extra layer of fear they face when it comes to their children, their sons, more specifically. The experiences of Black mothers facing threats to their sons from police violence have not been adequately investigated. As a result, we know very little about the experiences of a Black mother who fears her son's interactions with police officers. Black mothers have a story that is being ignored, a voice that is being silenced, and it is past time for them to be heard.

Purpose and Significance of the Study

This qualitative phenomenological study explored the lived experiences, and the meaning of Black motherhood as told by Black women, recognizing how they navigate their fears of potentially losing their sons during interactions with police officers. In addition, the study intended to contribute to the literature on the meaning and the lived experiences of the unique challenges Black mothers have raising and protecting one or more sons in a racial society. This study was conducted utilizing a Critical Race Theory (CRT) framework. CRT used in this research centered around the concept of counter-storytelling. Solórzano and Yosso (2002) assert that counter-storytelling is a method of telling the stories of those people whose experiences are not often told – those on the margins of society.

Furthermore, counter-storytelling is also a tool for analyzing, challenging, and exposing majoritarian stories of racial privilege (Bundles, 2015). For the study, this study drew from three essential CRT tenets. First, racism is normalized and deeply woven into the fabric of American society and its its institutions and can only be eradicated when named explicitly. Second, marginalized voices must be centered through storytelling, and third, affirming the experiential knowledge of the racism Black people endure at various levels is necessary to eradicate racism within systems and institutions (Delgado et al., 2012; Solórzano & Yosso, 2002). Naming the harm created by constructing Whiteness as the essence of normality while condemning Black people to the realm of inferiority is essential to understanding the creation of the group and race-based hierarchies in American society (McWhorter, 2005). The history of racism in the U.S. sheds light on the truths of racial injustice, while racialized issues of the past continue to pose challenges today. In addition, there is information provided on the existing research pertaining to the history of violence in the U.S. against Black males, with specific attention given to police racial bias and brutality. The research also showed the impact police brutality toward Black sons has on Black mothers' fear. Learning about Black mothers and the experiences these women have while raising Black boys is an essential step in addressing descriptions of Black families in the U.S. Finally, documenting Black mothers' lived experiences navigating their fears surrounding the possibility of losing their sons to police violence is critical to provide support in allowing Black women to utilize and maximize their voice in this experience.

Theoretical Framework

This study employed CRT as its theoretical framework. CRT is an intellectual movement that aims to comprehend the mechanisms by which White supremacy, as a legal, cultural, and political phenomenon, is perpetuated and upheld, predominantly within the social and legal framework of the U.S. (De La Garza & Ono, 2016). CRT aims to comprehend the underlying racial dynamics associated with social events that are often overlooked by both the public and academia, as well as society at large (Closson, 2010). In contrast, CRT is situated within a broader research tradition that explores the topics of race and racism. This tradition encompasses prominent scholars such as W. E. B. Du Bois, Frantz Fanon, Angela Davis, Audre Lorde, Gloria Anzaldúa, Cherrie Moraga, and others. CRT sets itself apart as an approach that emerged within the field of legal studies, drawing upon and addressing critical legal studies as a foundation. CRT aims to be a social and political change vehicle and has adopted interdisciplinarity across many fields, including education. In certain contexts, CRT has become the umbrella term for studies of race and racism in general (De La Garza & Ono, 2016).

CRT highlights the structural ways in which race is embedded in institutional systems, including law enforcement, reinforcing White power, and raising the possibility of treating minorities (i.e., African American males and other men of color) unfairly in order to maintain their inferior status in positions of power. The creator of the word "CRT," Kimberle Crenshaw, points out that CRT is a verb rather than a noun. It is regarded as a flexible and dynamic practice that cannot be limited to a rigid and static definition (George, 2021). It critiques how institutionalized racism, and the social construction of race perpetuate a racial caste system that demotes people of color to the lowest divisions. CRT acknowledges that racism is not an extinct relic of the past.

Instead, it recognizes that the enduring effects of slavery, segregation, and the marginalization of Black Americans and other people of color consistently permeate the societal structure of this nation (George, 2021).

Definition of Terms

African American - Refers to an individual whose ancestry can be traced back to Africa (Baruth & Manning, 2016) and who was unjustly transported to American soil. In power struggles or politics, the term "Black" typically encompasses all minority communities that are non-White (Comstock et al., 2004). The terms "Black" and "African American" are employed interchangeably in the context of this study.

Motherhood - Although there is no single meaning or given experience of motherhood (McMahon, 1995), women's roles as mothers are idealized in our culture as all-loving, kind, gentle, and selfless (Andersen, 1994). Motherhood is also the experience of being a mother.

Police brutality - "Refers to the utilization of disproportionate physical force, verbal attack, and psychological intimidation" (Walker, 2011, p. 579).

Police racial bias - Encompasses the practice of racial profiling of drivers, the presence of racial prejudices among law enforcement, and the unjust treatment of minority groups and communities (Weitzer & Tuch, 2005).

Racial bias - refers to the differential conduct exhibited by an individual that is associated with the race or ethnicity of another individual or group (National Academies of Sciences, Engineering, and Medicine, 2018).

Racial profiling - constitutes a type of discrimination

when law enforcement employs an individual's race, ethnicity, or national origin as a determining factor in their decision-making process regarding stops, searches, or detentions (Glaser, 2014). Profiling is an offense that infringes upon fundamental human rights, decreases trust within public institutions, and yields significant repercussions for both victims and society (Weizter & Tuch, 2002).

Racism - The belief in the superiority of one race over another, which often results in discrimination and prejudice towards people based on their race or ethnicity.

Research Question

The research question and methodology of this study were designed to explore the fears of Black mothers potentially losing sons to police brutality during encounters with police officers. The challenges that Black mothers experience while raising their sons also highlight the strengths and resiliency of Black mothers. Furthermore, this study provides a voice for Black mothers to share their experiences and fears of racial oppression.

There was one primary research question and three sections of interview questions that guided this research.

Research Question: How did Black mothers navigate their fears of potentially losing their sons during interactions with police officers?

Secondary Questions:
A. What were some of your most significant challenges in raising a male child?

B. What were your views about police officers overall?

C. Have you ever experienced racism or seen racial discrimination at the hands of police officers?

D. Have you tried to protect or educate your son about interactions with police officers?

E. What would you say are your strengths and resiliency as a Black mother raising sons in a racist society?

Chapter II

Literature Review

"Racism is man's gravest threat to man - the maximum of hatred for a minimum of reason." Abraham Heschel (1963)

History of Racism

To fully comprehend what it means to be an African American woman raising Black males in the U.S., one must first understand the stigmas and racial history within the U.S. that have both surrounded and dictated Black identity and treatment. Racism, prejudice, and discrimination have long been recognized and experienced by individuals who identify as "Black" in the U.S. The combined effect of brutality, bigotry, and violence, along with the utilization of painful and disembodying language, culminates in a synthesis of negativity, anguish, and distress. The Black community has been tormented by experiences of oppression, racism, and other repressive events for generations, starting from the beginning of American slavery in 1619 and continuing through the organized efforts to place inferior social statuses on Blacks during the Jim Crow era (Albach & Lomotey, 2002; Alexander, 1970). A traumatic and pervasive history of racism spans generations in the U.S., profoundly affecting the African American experience. Racism has had a long-lasting negative impact on African Americans that affects the mental, physical, emotional, and spiritual wellness of Black individuals and hinders access to healthcare, housing, and positive economic and financial outcomes (Graff, 2014). Religious, political, and economic liberty became the face and appeal of American society; however, American society was established on brutal forms of domination, inequality, and oppression, which involved the absolute denial of freedom for enslaved people (Wright, 2009). As a result, racism became a vital component of the American experience. It is challenging to define racism and comprehend the complex factors that surround a racist experience. When attempting to define or describe racism, it has been stated that it is difficult to pinpoint an all-inclusive definition.

According to Bonilla-Silva (2001), racism is frequently viewed as a form of prejudice, ignorance, or a pathological condition that occurs in specific individuals, leading them to engage in discriminatory behavior towards others based on their physical appearance. Racism is the act of subordinating individuals or groups based on race, which can manifest through policies, beliefs, attitudes, actions, or inactions (Salter et al., 2017). Given the particular historical development of racism as both an institution and an ideology spanning several centuries, Paula Rothenberg offers this more pointed and valuable definition of racism, especially in the current U.S. context: "Racism involves White people's subordination of people of color, and history provides a long record of White people holding and using power and privilege over people of color to subordinate them, not the reverse" (Wolf, n .d). In contrast, individual persons of color may discriminate against a White person or another person of color because of their race; that discrimination is prejudice; however, it does not qualify as racism because a person of color cannot depend upon the institutions of society to enforce or extend their dislike toward White people, nor can they call upon the force of history to reflect and enforce that prejudice. Throughout history, three distinct forms of racism have been identified: institutional racism, individual racism, and cultural racism (Katz & Taylor, 1988; Rutstein, 1997; Smith, 1995). Institutional racism involves the differential effects of laws, practices, and policies on members of certain racial groups, and it can develop from intentional racism; for example, limiting immigration based solely on the assumption that another group is inferior or providing resources to one's group in the attempt to restrict another group's voting power. Individual racism and prejudice exhibit similar distinguishing traits since they both center on the attitudes and actions of individuals toward others (Katz & Taylor, 1988).

These attitudes and actions are inherently harmful and driven by racial motivations. It causes certain types of behavior, including, but not limited to, White people projecting their ideas of inferiority onto Black people through prejudicial or discriminatory actions, and it is often enacted through the acceptance of stereotypical views or assumptions regarding Black people (Smith, 1995; Jones, 1988). While individual racism can have harmful consequences, cultural racism has a significant impact on the lives of millions of Black individuals, irrespective of their personal experiences with racism (Hudson, 1999). Cultural racism arises when a particular group exercises authority to establish cultural norms and values within a given society (Allport, 1954). Hence, the eradication of this issue poses significant challenges due to its deep roots within White culture, which perpetuates a negative assessment of Black culture (Katz & Taylor, 1988). This form of racism encompasses a preference for the cultural, historical, and moral aspects of one's group (ethnocentrism) and the imposition of this culture upon other people. In historical and modern societies, cultural racism has drawn growing recognition to racism and its manifestation in diverse domains such as physical attributes, societal norms, religious practices, moral convictions, artistic principles, customary rituals, recreational pursuits, and language (Halstead, 1988). For this reason, cultural racism involves being prejudiced and discriminatory against individuals because of their culture (Scott, 2007).

Modern Manifestation of Racism

Racism today is evident through hostile scenarios and behaviors toward specific groups based on race, ethnicity, and culture. Markers of these identities and various socio-political factors intersect with every aspect of racism to shape and transform racist expressions (Ben et al., 2020). Racism, religion, and xenophobic discrimination are not new and have been around for centuries in different structures and forms.

Our awareness and understanding of these social forces are new and enable our ability to predict when and why they occur (Lloyd, 2007; Paradies, 2016; Vertovec, 2007). Racist expressions and episodes have traveled across many countries, have translocated reach, and are disseminated rapidly due to the internet (Ben et al., 2020). Racism is a complex social issue, even more so today, as it permeates all aspects of daily life. In academic literature, modern racism is distinguished from traditional forms of racism based on specific groups perceived to have "biological" differences and superiority. Racism is recognized as a clear expression of hatred, contempt, and bias rooted in race or skin color (Elias, 2021). According to Gaertner and Dovidio (2005), modern racism encompasses a complex and subtle form of racism that primarily stems from cultural differences. It pertains to the complicated and occasionally implicit adverse beliefs about individuals primarily based on their racial or ethnic heritage. The focus has switched from the more "traditional" forms of racism, which were demonstrated by individuals' racial acts, discriminating words, and opposition against others, to policies that have the potential to promote equality (Garcia et al., 2016).

Racial prejudice encompasses various significant indicators such as race, ethnicity, skin color, culture, heritage, and nationality. Nevertheless, within this emerging version of racism, the biases and prejudices are concealed beneath the surface of statistical rationalism and the illusion of meritocracy (Brief et al., 2000). These biases are rarely evident to individuals who are not observant. Therefore, these manifestations of racism are sometimes referred to as unconscious bias by scholars (Banks & Ford, 2008). Since modern racism is not as blatant and is often expressed in publicly acceptable ways, it is easy to think that racism no longer exists. A few concepts can perpetuate contemporary racism and make it hard to identify and thus eliminate, these being aversive, symbolic, and modern racism.

Aversive racism occurs when an individual holds a negative bias against others based on their racial/ethnic background while believing that they support values of equality. Several people with aversive racism either claim to be against or honestly think they are against racism even though they have deeply held prejudices (Garcia et al., 2016). This manifestation of racism is frequently disregarded and can take various forms, such as an individual experiencing unease when in the presence of ethnic minorities, harboring unwarranted suspicions or doubts, and engaging in actions like avoidance. Symbolic racism, like aversive racism, pertains to entities that perpetuate the oppression of others. It entails a profound racial/ethnic prejudice manifested through the opposition of regulations, legislation, and principles that could benefit minority groups. Modern racism and symbolic racism are comparable in several ways, but modern racism holds an added view that racism is obsolete. The manifestation of modern racism is exemplified by individuals asserting their complete denial of biases and adopting a "colorblind" stance or contending that racism has become extinct in today's present era (Garcia et al., 2016).

Racial microaggressions, including microinsults, microassaults, and microinvalidations, are other forms of modern racism (Rodgers, 2015). Microaggression describes subtle communications of expectations and stereotypes relating to people of color. Microinsults are where someone is demeaning a person's racial heritage and identity; an example would be "subtle snubs" in which contributions made by people of color are unacknowledged, invisible, or marginalized. Micro-assaults are overtly racist and demeaning interactions, such as using a racial slur. Lastly, microinvalidations are where someone excludes, negates, and nullifies the psychological thoughts, feelings, or experiential reality of people of color (Rodgers, 2015).

Fears of Parenting within a Racist Society

Raising children has its difficulties and challenges regardless of race or ethnic background; however, raising kids who face possible daily assaults is even more complex and frightening for a parent. Tatum and Roberts (2020) tracked representative groups of mothers with kids from kindergarten to fourth grade nationwide. They found that Black mothers experience a higher level of parenting stress while their kids grow up. Their fears are centered around increasing their children's chances of survival and overall safety. Huggins et al. (2020) explored how dangerous the U.S. is for Blacks, finding that Blacks were almost eight times more likely than Whites to be homicide victims. Based on this data, one could argue that as a result, Black mothers are eight times as fearful as White mothers regarding their children's safety.

According to Malone Gonzalez (2019), weathering is a term used to describe the impacts of racism on Black mothers, worsening their health. For example, it is linked to a higher rate of diabetes and high blood pressure. Black mothers between the ages of 40 and 65 years are 50% more likely to suffer from high blood pressure, three times more likely to suffer from kidney failure, and 60% more likely to suffer from diabetes than White mothers. Malone Gonzalez noted that Black mothers are always on "high alert" regarding any chances of their children encountering unfair treatment. These stresses and factors potentially affect increasing inflammatory markers, slowing blood pressure recovery, and worsening sleep patterns. Huggins et al. (2020) highlighted that the images of Black deaths accelerated Black mothers' health deterioration and aging.

Racial inequality and racism thus have an enormous impact on the Black community, especially Black mothers, and their health. Their worries regarding their children and how to parent them in a racist and violent society that has historically shown its lack of care and support toward the Black community have an impact on their health. The seemingly never-ending hypervigilance that Black mothers experience adds to the decline of their mental and physical health, both things the Black community already struggles with due to the racially discriminatory environment created for them in the U.S. The deaths of Ahmaud Arbery and George Floyd are brutal reminders that regardless of how vigilant Black mothers are in protecting their children, it might not be sufficient to secure the safety of their children, especially when racism, prejudice, discrimination, and negative stereotypes are deep-rooted components that have affected Blacks for generations in the U.S. (Huggins et al., 2020).

History of Critical Race Theory (CRT)
Definition of CRT

CRT is a social and intellectual movement with a loosely organized legal framework based on the perception that races are not natural, nor are they biologically tagged features that physically differentiate human beings based on their color to justify oppression and exploitation. CRT holds that racism is intrinsic throughout the laws and legal institutions within the U.S. The U.S. creates and maintains political, economic, and social inequalities among people of different races, particularly between Whites and nonwhites. Because of this, CRT is dedicated to applying an institutional or structural understanding of the nature of racism to eliminate race-based or unjustified race hierarchy (Martinez, 2014).

How CRT Explains Racism

CRT explains racism as a socially constructed belief that is not based on biological truths or nature. Numerous genetic studies have disputed the idea of dividing human beings into distinct groups based on inherited behaviors. Many historians and social scientists have agreed that race is a social construction. CRT holds that race is an artificial correlation using skin color, hair texture, and facial characteristics to create a belief system that correlates those physical attributes to behavioral and psychological tendencies and perceives them as either positive or negative. This correlation has been perfectly executed and practiced by White people in the U.S. and other Western countries to perpetuate oppression and exploitation of other groups due to perceived inferiority and immorality. CRT also explains racism within the aspect of "material determinism" or "interest convergence," in which setbacks for people of color serve the interest of the dominant group or White people (Donner et al., 2018).

CRT and Racism - Implications on the Treatment of Young Black Men

Using CRT, the challenges young Black men face when interacting with the police can be further analyzed and explained. Ideally, we should live in a post-racial society that no longer believes in or perpetuates negative stereotypes involving Black people, particularly Black men, and their assumed involvement with criminal activity before proper investigation. However, there is still a very evident belief system in the U.S. that supports mistreatment and negative behavior regarding Black men and criminal activity that still has an invisible touch of racism (Martinez, 2014). It is still seen and experienced between Black men and police today, even though it is often mistakenly emphasized as something that no longer exists. CRT is against the denial of racism and racialized relationships that prevent reasonable actions from being made against racism. Institutions should inextricably link histories of racism and control the antithetical function of the police to lead to equity in practice. CRT recognizes the history and development of institutionalized racism and strives to re-imagine Black people as victims rather than suspects. CRT names racism as a vital step in speaking the truth about the constant fight for power and superiority, as well as the importance of accepting the adverse effects racism inevitably creates, which society enables.

While this racist system has undergone substantial alterations throughout the centuries (Feagin, 2006), systemic racism has dramatically escalated in the U.S. criminal justice system through the slaying of many unarmed Black men by police officers, leading to unprecedented fears of police victimization (Tobin-Tyler, 2021). Even though most parents have said that everything has become a teaching moment for their sons, Black parents find it difficult to teach their children that it is okay to walk around their neighborhood, as well as allow their kids the necessary freedom to explore the world around them, due to the fear of unjust treatment looming everywhere they go (Tyler, 2022). The saying "let kids be kids" is entirely different for Black sons since they are likely to face mistreatment or brutality of some kind within society (Rogers, 2015). Young Black men, particularly those residing in poor communities, are subjected to interrogation and arrest by police officers at a higher rate than young White men.

Encounters with police officers are frequent among poor young Black individuals since most of them are stopped and searched by police officers, deeming their behavior as "routine" (Malone Gonzalez, 2019). Both empirical studies and federal investigations have reported the unconstitutional tormenting of Black men and women by police (Tatum, 2017). Investigations by the U.S. Department of Justice throughout several U.S. cities showed that police officers used brutal force more severely and frequently with Black men (Tatum, 2017).

Such disparities are pervasive among Black men. These police practices lead to a total violation of civil liberties for Black men, placing them at a disproportionate risk of violent injuries or death when they encounter police (Desmond et al., 2016).

Black males are prone to being stereotyped and are stigmatized as hypersexual, aggressive, and more likely to commit a crime or be involved in criminal activities (Ashley, 2021). In addition, Social Dominance Theory (SDT) elucidates that Black men in low-status groups experience more bias than Black women since they are depicted as a threat to the racial hierarchy (Ashley, 2021; Rogers, 2015). Deadly encounters arise when law enforcement trains their police officers to be aggressive and apply hostile masculinity through implicit and explicit racial bias and combative personalities (Rogers, 2015). Thus, young men should be educated about the dangers of racism in their interactions with police, and this task is often left up to their parents to teach them (Rogers, 2015).

History of Police Brutality Towards Black Americans

Today, police brutality is all too common. In recent years, the U.S. has witnessed unrest involving people of color and the killings of unarmed Black men at the hands of police officers. We are confronted with horrific images and stories through news outlets and social media that can be difficult to understand and process. Police brutality in the U.S. cannot be discussed without confronting the racism and racial profiling that reinforces it. Police brutality encompasses a spectrum of actions, including physical assault, such as beatings, as well as acts of violence, torture, and homicide. In addition, police brutality can be expanded to include many other forms of harassment, such as false arrest, intimidation, and verbal abuse (Moore, 2020). Police brutality has affected individuals of all races, ethnicities, ages, classes, and genders in the U.S., however, there has been a notable disproportionate number of Black victims (Moore, 2020). Racialized policing has existed in America ever since the country's first state-sponsored police force was established, commonly known as slave patrols. According to Ritchie and Mogul (2008), the origins of racial profiling and police brutality can be traced back to the enforcement of Slave Codes, followed by Black Codes and Jim Crow segregation legislation. As an illustration, the petition "We Charge Genocide," which was presented to the United Nations (U.N.) by the Civil Rights Congress in 1951, recorded numerous incidents of police brutality explicitly targeting Black individuals (Ritchie & Mogul, 2016).

Official studies, along with domestic and international civil and human rights organizations, have routinely found that communities predominantly occupied by Black people, or people of color in general, are excessively subjected to human rights violations at the hands of police officers. These offenses encompass a broad spectrum, including widespread harassment and verbal abuse, routine stop-and-frisks, racial profiling purely based on race or gender, insufficient use of force, unwarranted shootings, and torture (Ritchie & Mogul, 2016). The American populace witnessed such a violation of life in May of 2020 when, for 9 minutes and 46 seconds, Derek Chauvin pressed his knee into the neck of George Floyd, an unarmed Black man.

The now-former Minneapolis police officer's deadly use of force has reignited a public debate about police brutality and racism (Peeples, 2020). According to Schwartz (2020), George Floyd is among the many instances of police killings that occurred in the year 2020. American law enforcement statistics exhibit staggering disparities compared to other developed countries (Schwartz, 2020). Among Black Americans, there is a significantly greater incidence of fatal police shootings compared to other ethnic groups, with a rate of 30 fatal shootings per million as of June 2020 (Schwartz, 2020).

Furthermore, according to the Statista Research Department (2021), the trend of fatal police shootings in the U.S. seems to be increasing, with a total of 604 civilians being shot, 108 of which were Black, in the first six months of 2021. In 1963, Martin Luther King Jr. stated, "They are asking civil rights devotees, 'When will you be satisfied?' As long as Negroes continue to suffer from the unspeakable atrocities of police brutality, we will never be satisfied" (Chaney & Davis, 2015, p. 269). This message echoes into present times after a lengthy past of brutal encounters between Black Americans and police. Pretzer (2019), the Smithsonian Museum senior history curator, expressed, "This idea of police brutality was on people's minds in 1963, following the years and decades of police abusing their power and then centuries of oppression of African Americans" (Pretzer, 2019). In March 1991, four officers were caught on videotape beating Rodney King, a Black man, after a high-speed chase through Los Angeles, California. The video and results that followed frightened the city and horrified the nation. Police brutality being caught on camera for everyone to see and witness forever altered discussions about race and policing in the U.S.; as technology evolves, it brings the issue of police brutality to light. Although the technology documenting police abuse is relatively new, the underlying problem is not. The killings of Michael Brown, Oscar Grant, Stephon Clark, Tamir Rice, George Floyd, and many other unarmed African American men are prime examples.

The protests following these killings have brought national attention to the racialized character of police violence against civilians, particularly Black Americans. As a result of police brutality becoming more evident and less deniable across the country, Black Lives Matter, a nationwide movement, was developed to challenge police brutality, demand police reform, and represent the human rights struggle for Black people (Tometi & Lenoir, 2015). Black Lives Matter has continued to draw national attention and has been a front-line movement demanding justice and accountability around state violence and police brutality against Black people.

Racial Disparities in Police Brutality

The underlying driver of racial disparity in police brutality is excessive policing in Black communities, often brought by legitimate wrongdoings. For instance, stop-and-frisk encounters disproportionately impact Black communities, but only 3% of the incidents have proof of criminal activity (Hollis & Jennings, 2018). This treatment by police often breeds a lack of trust in law enforcement in Black communities, resulting in certain doubts, such as not believing in the legitimacy of law enforcement and not reporting crimes (Hollis & Jennings, 2018). These racially biased tactics do not build a more robust and safer community but begin to erode trust among communities, especially between young people and the police. This erosion of trust inevitably leads to an unconscionable victimization rate among Black males by law enforcement (Hollis & Jennings, 2018). Unfortunately, racial disparities are rising and are becoming more deeply rooted in the legal system. For example, under Stop-and-Frisk, a police procedure, security personnel have the liberty to stop people based on the "legitimate suspicions" of criminal activities that such people are armed and dangerous (Tobin-Tyler, 2021; Waldron, 2020). The New York City Police Department made more than four million stops along the streets, and close to 80% of these stops were Black people, (Huggins et al., 2020;

Rogers, 2015). This Stop-and-Frisk policy has made the practice of stopping individuals who seem suspicious a controversial topic of concern since 1968. Although the Supreme Court approved it, as they did in the Terry v. Ohio case of 1968, it unfortunately seems to advance racial disparities and reflects community tension while perpetuating disconnects between law enforcement officers and the Black community (Rogers, 2015; Tyler, 2022).

Black Mothers Experience Racism and Police Brutality

Recent studies suggest that police brutality may contribute to various consequences for Black people's mental health (Malone Gonzalez, 2019; Roberts, 2011). Black mothers undergo traumatic circumstances when law enforcement brutally kills their sons. The mental health of these mothers is always affected by the heinous killings of their loved ones without apparent reason. For example, researchers found that Black mothers residing in places where there are killings of unarmed people happened to experience a greater number of mental health issues overall than White mothers living in the same locality (Desmond et al., 2016).

Additionally, Black Americans are subjected to publicized instances of police killings by the media. In turn, these publicized events increase the fear of state agents and cause legitimate concern for their safety and fear of death that can be inflicted by police officers (Roberts, 2011). The relationship between mental health and aggressive policing showed that intrusive police stops predicted a greater prevalence of post-traumatic stress disorder (PTSD) for Black mothers than for White mothers (Tatum, 2017). Exposure to police brutality exacerbates an imperative event in the lives of Black mothers (Roberts, 2011).

The Diagnostic and Statistical Manual of Mental Disorders (DSM-5-TR) defines trauma as exposing human beings to threats or actual death, severe injuries, or sexual violence. An individual can directly or indirectly suffer from trauma. For example, if one were told that their loved ones had experienced an act of violence resulting in a trauma response, they may be at high risk for experiencing trauma themselves. Black mothers experience aversive trauma when their sons are exposed to police killings or police violence in the community (Hilton, 2005; Tatum, 2017). Exposure to trauma leads to the production of psychological arousals, negative moods, avoidance, and cognition that experience PTSD development or trauma-associated disorders (Desmond et al., 2016). While people exposed to trauma do not meet specific diagnostic PTSD criteria, trauma exposure always induces vulnerability and a sense of fear (Huggins et al., 2020).

Racial disparities in U.S. policing elucidate exposure to police killings and police violence as chronic and trauma stressors in Black mothers' lives (Desmond et al., 2016). Hilton (2005) theorized through the cognitive appraisal model that stressors are experienced when events are assumed to be stressful, exceeding assumed resources to handle the perceived stressors. Black Americans, and Black males particularly, assume threats of violent victimization by police officers (Hilton, 2005; Roberts, 2011) since it is a disparate source of stress (Desmond et al., 2016).

Black Mothers' Impact of Possibly Losing Their Son to Police Brutality

After realizing that their kids are experiencing unfair treatment and are more vulnerable, Black mothers may change their parenting strategies to ensure their children are safe. These strategies comprise "The Talk," which is a necessary talk that Black parents, mainly mothers, give their children, particularly their sons, about how they deal with police if they encounter them. For instance, strict supervision using chaperonage and family support from uncles and other family members may be required (Desmond et al., 2016; Rogers, 2015). Some Black mothers are ready to ignore the conventional parenting structure, where kids are brought up in close monitoring with their parents and guardians; instead, they utilize exile strategies, where young children are sent away from their communities to spend time with their distant relatives for their safety (Desmond et al., 2016). Parents of Black sons commonly utilize exile since they are mainly focused on protecting their children from police brutality (Desmond et al., 2016). Homicide is one of the leading causes of death for Black sons between 16 and 35 (Desmond et al., 2016). For Black sons in the U.S., the probability of being killed is about 15 times that of White teenagers (Rogers, 2015).

Nevertheless, the fear of death for Black sons comes from the violence within the community and their mothers' fears that their sons could easily experience violent brutality by the police (Rogers, 2015). Many African American mothers narrated their experiences and perceptions to researchers about how police interact with their families and communities (Rogers, 2015). They consistently adapted to police brutality and implemented new ways of protecting their sons to combat personal and structural interactions with the police (Rogers, 2015). The police relationship with the community is often quite apprehensive, and the Black community faces the full wrath of police actions. This suggests that Black mothers exhibit higher levels of fear compared to White mothers, even when they are in similar environments.

Mothers' Grief

The process of finding meaning is still disregarded for Black mothers, who are disproportionately impacted by loss relating to homicide. This can cause disruptive psychological trauma and even leave them struggling with several adaptive challenges (Bailey et al., 2013). Undoubtedly, the experience of losing a child is profoundly challenging. The apprehension of losing a child to violence is deeply unsettling for African American women. According to Johnson (2016), the Black Women's Health Imperative has identified that African American women can develop symptoms of PTSD because of their exposure to racially motivated incidents and continuous exposure to violent or harmful media. Black mothers act as a unit. When one of them loses a child, they all experience hurt through racial violence, implying that vicarious trauma is a critical aspect of a Black mother's experience. These mothers are faced with murders like that of Michael Brown and Stephon Clark, unarmed Black men who interacted with armed police officers (Huggins et al., 2020). It is a sad twist of fate that Black mothers must carry these worries around, constantly fearing that their child will become the next Stephon Clark, Michael Brown, or George Floyd (Huggins et al., 2020). These symptoms are heightened in women who experience the loss of their children due to acts of violence (Johnson, 2016). Grieving a child's loss at the hands of police violence is a unique gut-wrenching experience that African American mothers have dealt with and continue to deal with today.

There is an expectation for Black mothers to exhibit strength and suppress their feelings, even in the face of persistent media coverage and widespread protests and demonstrations occurring in different areas across the nation (Johnson, 2016). These mothers often engage with individuals who lack the capacity to comprehend their experiences, exhibit hesitancy in allowing them to express their perspectives, refrain from demonstrating empathy, and neglect to offer preventive interventions. Overwhelming stress can result from these events, leading to feelings such as isolation, fear, and worry (Lawson, 2018). In one of the studies, a participant expressed that upon being informed of a recent incident of police shooting following the unfortunate death of their child because of police violence, she anticipated experiencing physical illness. In addition, another participant reported instances of stomach distress, insomnia, and heart palpitations.

An important theme emerges when examining the experiences of Black mothers. Research conducted throughout history demonstrates that African American mothers who have been forced to raise their sons in violent situations and have experienced the loss of their sons because of violence experience adverse effects on their physical, emotional, and mental well-being. Grief is a feeling many are familiar with and have experienced in one way or another throughout their lives; however, grief is only the beginning for Black mothers who have lost their children due to unnecessary violence.

Black Motherhood

A focus on what Black mothers feel, think, and carry concerning the possibility of losing their Black sons would be a pressing issue, especially with all the systemic challenges Black men face to fit in or survive in our society. Watson and Hunter (2016) note that the idea of the 'strong Black woman schema' is a stereotypical perception that the Black woman needs to show strength and courage in the face of pain. It may promote stability and caretaking, which is also a central aspect of African womanhood; however, Black women are often forced to internalize their pains and the intersectionality of their oppressions and adversities, often leading to many health-related issues (Watson & Hunter, 2016). Moreover, the pains, fears, and hopelessness Black women face can be seen in the early socialization of their children on race and discrimination-related issues. As Edwards and Few-Demo (2016) point out, Black mothers engage in the racial socialization process with their children from preschool to enlighten them on the implications of racial differentials and how to cope when they see the police. This practice has become a norm among African American mothers who are compelled to negotiate powerlessness and fear on how to protect their children from systemic oppression and police violence (Edwards & Few-Demo, 2016). Despite the fear of police violence and indiscriminate killings, it is essential to recognize that Black women also face discrimination and must navigate racism, sexism, and patriarchy themselves, coupled with trying to be heard in situations of systemic injustices concerning themselves and their sons.

As Pratt-Clarke (2013) points out, "There are also many unwritten and unspoken practices that affect the experiences of African American women, and some of the critical challenges is learning, unearthing, uncovering, and challenging what is unwritten and unspoken, yet acted upon" (p. 101). Pratt-Clarke (2013) correlates how various aspects of oppression intersect in educational systems, the legal system, the political system, and the criminal justice system. These components conjunctively affect interactions with other individuals and groups. Moreover, intersecting identities, including race, gender, and class, within these interpersonal relationships become salient. As a result, these identities often influence and determine the respect, power, prominence, and authority Black women receive (Pratt-Clarke, 2013). Therefore, it is important to examine the narratives of Black girls and women so that instances of injustices and oppression can be unearthed, unsilenced, made visibly acknowledged, and recognized (Pratt-Clarke, 2013). Bailey et al. (2013) do just that, outlining the cognitive process of finding meaning and building resilience after losing a child to gun violence. Bailey points out that the loss of a child is a traumatic experience that can leave parents in a state of trepidation, whereby they cannot find meaning in their loss. For Black mothers, who are disproportionately affected by loss through homicide, the process of making meaning remains overlooked. This can cause disruptive psychological trauma and even leave them struggling with several adaptive challenges (Bailey et al., 2013).

    Overall, previous scholarly work shows a historical trend of prejudice, discrimination, and racism toward the African American community – a trend that began with slaves arriving in Jamestown in 1619 and continuing through the present day, with several high-profile murders of young Black men just in the past few years. This racism by design has had a significantly negative impact on Black communities. However, there also exists a need for more in-depth study on the lived experiences and effects of Black mothers, particularly regarding the challenges they face raising young Black men in the U.S., the effects that racism has on their respective lives, and the mitigation strategies they employ to navigate an inequitable world. That said, this study's primary research question, how did Black mothers navigate their fears of potentially losing their sons during interactions with police officers, sought to address this gap in literature.

Chapter III

Methods

This study utilized a phenomenological approach of qualitative research methodology to explore the lived experiences of African American mothers' fears of potentially losing their sons during interactions with police officers. This methodology was selected because there was an interest in capturing the lived experiences of a group of individuals, particularly regarding how they interpret the phenomenon they experience. The following sections provide descriptions of the methodological procedures used in this study. In the first section of this chapter, I describe a phenomenological approach. The second section highlights the transcendental phenomenology to be used in this study. Following this, the third section explains transcendental phenomenology according to Van Kaam's guiding principles. The fourth section includes the recruitment procedures, participants' inclusion criteria, protection of participants, sample size, and gaining access to the participants. The fifth section describes the process of data collection, and the sixth section presents the procedures of the data analysis plan. The final section delves into the transferability, credibility, dependability, and confirmability of this study and summarizes the chapter.

Phenomenological Approach

Van Manen (1990) defined phenomenology as a depiction of the lived-through quality of lived experiences. On the one hand, it is the "immediate description of life, whereas, on the other hand, it is the mediated description of the lifeworld as expressed in a symbolic form" (p.25). Patton (2002) and Descombe (2003) described the ordinary meaning of phenomenology as depicting and analyzing the meaning of the lived experiences of individuals.

Furthermore, Patton (2002) stated that phenomenology is about interpreting "how participants perceive a phenomenon, describe it, feel about it, judge it, remember it, make sense of it, and talk about it with others" (p. 104). Additionally, Todres and Holloway (2004) illustrated a similar goal of phenomenology in which "people who have experienced a phenomenon can communicate their perceptions to the outside world and therefore answer questions of meaning in understanding and experience from those who have experienced it" (p. 215). Rossman (2006) and Creswell (2007) described a phenomenological approach as one of the most effective ways of interpreting a person's lived experiences for an in-depth understanding of the phenomenon and to express participants' accounts.

This research is framed in the CRT theoretical framework to understand how Black mothers process fear of racial oppression from their lived experiences. Therefore, the research goal was to understand and interpret how the participants process the meaning of the fears of potentially losing their sons during interactions with police officers. As phenomenology is used primarily to describe the experiences of an individual or a group of people, this type of approach is considered suitable for the context of this study because it seeks to interpret a particular phenomenon and bring meaning to it.

Transcendental Phenomenology
There are several approaches available for structuring

and analyzing data in phenomenological qualitative research. Husserl (1931) initially formulated the transcendental phenomenology framework, which Moustakas (1994) then modified into a qualitative research approach. This framework demonstrates promise as an appropriate instrument for phenomenological research (Moerer-Urdahl & Creswell, 2004). Transcendental phenomenology "embraces the qualitative focus on the wholeness of experience, search for essences of experiences, and viewing experience and behavior as an integrated and inseparable relationship of subject and object" (Raffanti, 2008, p. 59). Consistent with the Husserlian approach, transcendental phenomenology provides a means to understand the essence of a phenomenon, making every effort to remove the researcher's subjective experiences, assumptions, and ideals to focus purely on the experiences of those experiencing the phenomenon (Moustakas, 1994). To do this, the researcher must transcend his or her biases and assumptions to see the phenomenon "freshly, as for the first time," and be open to its totality (Moustakas, 1994, p. 34). Transcendental phenomenology is most useful when "the researcher has identified a phenomenon to understand and have individuals who can describe what they have experienced" (Moerer-Urdahl & Creswell, 2004, p. 32).

The literature on transcendental phenomenology suggests that there are core processes of connectivity interwoven with lived experience (Husserl, 1931, 1954; Moustakas, 1994). In other words, one's mind is oriented to an object through varying frames (e.g., perspectives) and is inseparable from thought to the object (Moustakas, 1994, p. 22). Through this research method, varying frames are then transitioned into the narrative by filling in contextual gaps (Maree, 2015; Smith et al., 2015). This constitutes the meaning of the lived experience from the invariant elements (Moustakas, 1994, p. 144). By this means, the essence can be uncovered from the natural world through transcendental phenomenology through an intentional experience of cognitive bracketing and open-ended interviews (Moustakas, 1994). Moustakas (1994) suggested an "intentional experience incorporates real content and ideal content" (p. 44).

Participants

This study's aim was to gain a deeper understanding of how Black mothers navigate their fears of potentially losing their sons during interactions with police officers. A target sample of 10 participants was utilized for this study. The participants in this study all identified as African American adult females over 18 years of age, with at least one Black male child, although some participants may have more than one son. Furthermore, participants in this study were biological, step, or adoptive mothers. In addition to fulfilling the inclusion criteria mentioned above, it was crucial to choose participants who had firsthand experience with the phenomenon being studied, were eager to comprehend its essence, were willing to engage in a lengthy recorded interview, and consented to the research being published in a dissertation (Moustakas, 1994). Therefore, the selected participants all met these criteria as well.

Protection of Participants

Qualitative research involves the establishment of trust, the recognition of mutuality, the maintenance of positive connections, and the sensitive acknowledgment of ethical considerations. Participant protection was implemented in this research study to safeguard the rights of the participants. I wanted to create an environment in which participants felt safe and supported as they described their lived experiences navigating fears of potentially losing their sons during interactions with police officers.

Following Alliant International University's IRB's approval of the Institutional Review Board (IRB) application (IRB-AY2022-2023-344), more precautions were implemented to safeguard the participants. The details and expectations of the study have been comprehensively outlined in the consent form for potential participants. After the African American mothers agreed to participate, their signatures were obtained on the consent form. Additionally, I emphasized that participation in the study was optional and that participants could withdraw from the research at any time without incurring any negative consequences. Each participant was given a copy of the signed consent form. Methods included face-to-face video-recorded interviews, demographic questionnaires, and field notes. Interview times ranged from one and a half to two hours to complete. I conducted this study virtually via the Zoom teleconferencing application, and all the participants were located within the U.S. Participants completed a demographic questionnaire prior to recorded interviews, in which they provided data regarding their age, gender, racial/ethnic identity, number and gender of their children, relational status, the highest level of education, employment, and income. No one else but the interviewer was present during the interviews; however, participants were given the option to have someone else present. The recorded information was kept confidential, and no one except Tatiana Glebova, Dissertation Chair, and two peers who verified the accuracy of my codes and themes accessed the information documented during interviews.

Furthermore, a minimum of three counseling referrals

were made available to all participants if they required such assistance, given the sensitive nature of the subject matter. To the best of my ability, participant confidentiality was maintained throughout this study. After each interview, the video recordings were transcribed and stored on a password-protected thumb drive. A second copy of the recordings was stored on a password-protected thumb drive in a secure secondary location as a backup if the primary copy was destroyed.

The records, information, and data will be destroyed within five (5) years of signing the consent form. I also told participants I was happy to share the findings with them after the research was completed. Consent forms/demographic information and recorded interviews were stored separately. The consent forms and demographic information were locked in a secure file cabinet, and recordings were stored on a password-protected thumb drive.

Sampling Procedures

This study covers a sensitive topic. To ensure participants, several techniques to recruit participants were used. Participants for this study were recruited through word-of-mouth from friends, co-workers, and classmates who shared my study to recruit participants. The flyer criteria included potential participants to identify as Black females must be biological, step or adoptive mothers, 18 years of age and older, English speakers, and U.S. residents. Additionally, flyers were distributed on social media (Facebook and Instagram) to Black women's support groups (Black Mamas Matter Alliance and Mother Against Police Brutality), and Black churches were employed to recruit participants. Furthermore, snowball sampling was also used to recruit participants. According to Marshall and Rossman (2016), snowball sampling is a type of sampling in which present participants enlist the assistance of their acquaintances to become future participants. Those who replied to my flyer were asked if they knew of anyone who might be interested in taking part in this study and met the inclusion criteria. Snowball sampling proved to be a highly efficient approach for this study, mainly when it is challenging to enlist people with the desired criteria.

Data Collection Methods

The data collection methods employed in this study included a demographic questionnaire, a face-to-face video-recorded interview, and field notes.

Demographic Questionnaire

Before the interview process, participants completed a demographic questionnaire. The full text of the questionnaire is listed in Appendix C.

Face-to-Face Video-Recorded Interview

Individual face-to-face semi-structured interviews in qualitative research are essential for building rapport and gaining rich and in-depth information and variable opinions compared to a group interview, in which one's opinion may be changed by the answers of others and result in similar responses (Merriam & Grenier, 2019). The transcendental phenomenological approach was considered when choosing an interview protocol to gain a deeper understanding of how Black mothers navigate their fears of potentially losing their sons during interactions with police officers. The interview process included a face-to-face, video-recorded interview using a Zoom conferencing platform. Follow-up questions and clarifying statements for participants were provided when necessary or to ask for clarification.

Interview Procedures

After recruiting my target sample of participants, the participants agreed upon a day, time, and location for the interviews. While I preferred to conduct all interviews in person due to the study's sensitivity, the participants opted to do the interviews via Zoom. To honor their request, all interviews were conducted virtually through a Zoom conferencing platform. The interviews were conducted in a private, quiet room of the participants' choice and were video-recorded and then transcribed verbatim by the researcher. Video recordings and transcriptions were stored on a password-protected thumb drive.

Data Analysis Plan

According to Merriam and Grenier (2019), data analysis involves integrating and summarizing textual and descriptive data acquired during the data collection to apply an understanding of the phenomenon studied, which can be communicated to others. Transcendental phenomenology emphasizes the researcher's involvement in clarifying the phenomenon through reflection as the subject perceives, describes, and experiences it (Merriam & Grenier, 2019; Moustakas, 1994). Moustakas' (1994) modified Van Kaam data analysis was applied in this transcendental phenomenological study to explain how Black mothers navigate their fears of potentially losing their sons during interactions with police officers. Coding was conducted using electronic software. The video-recorded interviews were transcribed verbatim into Microsoft Word documents. The transcripts were imported as source files into NVivo 14 computer-assisted qualitative data analysis software. The modification of the Van Kaam approach for interpreting phenomenological data proposed by Moustakas (1994) encompassed a series of eight distinct procedures. According to Sullivan and Bhattacharya (2017), the modified Van Kaam data analysis procedure was systematically used to apply participant data at each stage. The following steps modify the Van Kaam analysis technique: the processes involved are horizontalization, reduction, elimination, identification, thematizing, validation, individual textual description, and textural and structural description.

Horizontalization is the initial step of the modified Van Kaam data analysis approach. This requires listing all relevant expressions related to the individual's life experience and assigning equal importance to each statement (Moustakas, 1994). The next step involves the process of reduction and elimination. This entails identifying invariant aspects and assessing whether the language comprehends the phenomenon, which can be referred to as a horizon of the lived experience (Moustakas, 1994). The third step of re-reading and analyzing each narrative involves identifying specific phrases or expressions that describe a fundamental component of the experience. According to Moustakas (1994), the fundamental components of the experience are abstract claims that converge towards a common theme, which may be found either implicitly or explicitly in most narratives. The fourth step in the data analysis entails organizing similar invariant elements into thematic labels, which emerge as core themes within the experience (Moustakas, 1994). According to Moustakas (1994), the fourth step of the data analysis procedure involves organizing comparable invariant elements into thematic labels, which subsequently emerge as key themes within the experience. The fifth step is application validation, wherein the significant themes are cross-referenced with the complete transcript to determine their explicit expression and compatibility. If these themes are not found, they are then deleted (Moustakas, 1994). To proceed, it is necessary to obtain "evidence from the participant's own words" (Grumstrup & Demchak, 2019, p. 118). In other words, are the participant responses relevant to the central themes? If not, one or more themes must be eliminated. In the six steps, it is necessary to construct a distinct textual description of the experience for each participant's interview transcription, utilizing the confirmed themes (Moustakas, 1994). The seven steps entail creating structural descriptions for each participant's comprehensive experience that originated from the previously built textual description. Additionally, these descriptions incorporate imaginative variation, as Moustakas (1994) suggested. The last step involves generating a textural-structural description of each participant's experience, effectively communicating the fundamental nature and significance of the experiences, encompassing the invariant components and themes (Moustakas, 1994).

Prior phenomenological research has employed the modified Van Kaam data analysis method for identifying themes, connections, and relationships among participants' experiences (Anthony & Weide, 2015; Grumstrup & Demchak, 2019; Mpuang et al., 2015). The data analysis method for this study allowed me to establish themes from the data collected to describe the essence and meaning of Black mothers' fears of potentially losing their sons during interactions with police officers.

Trustworthiness

According to Ohri (2021), qualitative research differs from quantitative research in that it does not incorporate statistical tests for assessing reliability and validity. Nevertheless, methods exist to determine the confidence of the "truth" in the study's findings. The "confidence trustworthiness" concept encompasses four distinct criteria: credibility, transferability, dependability, and confirmability (Sutton & Austin, 2015). Researchers who prioritize trustworthiness in their work can effectively safeguard the integrity of their findings and conclusions (Korstjens and Moser, 2018).

Credibility

Credibility refers to the extent to which the research findings accurately reflect the information obtained from the participants' original data and accurately interpret their original perspectives (Graneheim & Lundman, 2004; Lincoln & Guba, 1985). Peer debriefing is a crucial factor concerning credibility, as it helps the researcher critically reflect on their research design and role throughout the inquiry (Creswell, 2013; Creswell & Miller, 2000; Houghton et al., 2013; Lincoln & Guba, 1985). To enhance the credibility of my study, I selected two doctoral candidates who are peers to analyze two out of the ten transcribed interviews. Their purpose was to provide meaningful feedback on the themes that arose from an in-depth examination of the data and the initial code classification. My peers pointed out areas where a theme or code description may have been too vague, allowing me to modify. This input aimed to strengthen the verification of my research. My peers validated the accuracy of my codes and themes. This enabled me to further examine my methodology and the interpretation of data to prevent personal bias.

Furthermore, the member checks can potentially increase the study's credibility (Bloomberg & Volpe, 2012; Merriam, 2009; Yin, 2014). The method of member checking involves the researcher giving the participants a summary of their data and interpretations so they can amend or validate the interpretations for validation (Belotto, 2018). To further credibility, I also invited the participants to make further comments on their interviews and reject interpretations made by the researcher that might be inaccurate (Schwandt et al., 2007). Before summarizing my collected data, two out of the ten participants offered additional comments on their interviews. P1 elaborated on the difficulties associated with being a Black mother and raising a Black child, while P8 provided further details regarding her efforts to educate her son regarding encounters with law enforcement. The two participants attest that their experiences in the transcribed interviews are entirely accurate.

Transferability

Transferability refers to whether the findings of a study can be adapted to other scenarios and contexts (Noble & Smith, 2015). Transferability is essential in research as it establishes a structure for future research, the practical implementation of research findings, and the evaluation of research outcomes (Cope, 2014) in the hope that more studies on various aspects of how African American mothers navigate their fears of potentially losing their sons during interactions with police officers would be replicated. Within my study, I ensured transferability by thoroughly explaining my research methodology, procedure, data collection procedures, and analysis with clarity and accuracy. To enhance the transferability of their findings, qualitative researchers can employ comprehensive descriptions of their findings to illustrate their applicability to different conditions, contexts, or situations (Carminati, 2018). To increase the transferability of my research,

I have provided comprehensive explanations of my findings, enabling other researchers and readers to discover potential avenues for future transferability.

Dependability

Dependability shows how the study's findings are consistent and may be repeated. Dependability includes participants' interpretation, evaluation of the findings, and recommendations of the study are supported by the data received from informants of the study (Cohen et al., 2011; Tobin & Begley, 2004). Researchers ensure dependability when their research findings exhibit consistent and stable results, allowing future researchers to apply the same framework or obtain similar results (Yin, 2018). To establish dependability in this study, I employed members checking where participants verified the accuracy of the interview data. Additionally, peer evaluations were conducted during data analysis to further verify dependability.

Confirmability

Confirmability, as defined by Belotto (2018), pertains to the degree to which a study's findings can be verified or supported by others, solely relying on the replies given by participants without being impacted by the researcher's personal biases or objectives (Belotto, 2018). According to Cope (2014), this ensures that the study's findings are derived from data and information without being impacted by personal motivations or biases. I ensured confirmability by keeping a reflexive journal in which I documented values, interests, biases, and personal experiences. I also reflected on my background and position. The trustworthiness of this transcendental phenomenological research study establishes its credibility, dependability, and confirmability. These components are crucial in demonstrating the robustness and trustworthiness of qualitative data.

Chapter IV

Results

Each participant met the inclusion criteria for this study. The participants consisted of ten mothers; their ages ranged from 31 to 61. All ten women identified as Black and biological mothers to their sons. All ten mothers and their sons were born in the U.S. The participants' sons all identify as Black; their ages range from 7 to 42. Out of the ten participants, three of the mothers have never been married, three are currently married, and four are divorced. All the participants are either college graduates or have some college experience. Eight out of the ten participants are gainfully employed, and two are retired. Participants described their socioeconomic status as high to middle class.

Table 1
Demographic Information

P	Age	# of Sons	Relational Status	Education	Employment
1	39	2	Never Married	BA	Nursing Assistant
2	54	5	Divorced	AA	Caterer
3	41	2	Divorced	MA	Response Therapist
4	40	1	Never Married	AA	Realtor
5	49	2	Married	MA	Marriage/Family Therapist
6	31	1	Never Married	MS	Registered Nurse
7	54	1	Divorced	BA	Government Analyst
8	59	1	Divorced	Some/College	Retired
9	51	1	Married	BA	Insurance Agent
10	61	2	Married	Some/College	Retired

Findings

The purpose of this chapter was to present the findings that emerged from executing the data collection and data analysis procedures described in Chapter Three. The following section of this chapter is a description of how the modified Van Kaam data analysis procedure was applied to the one-to-one, semi-structured interview data from the 10 Black mother participants. The research question developed to guide this study was: How do Black mothers navigate their fears of potentially losing their sons during interactions with police officers? This chapter then proceeds with a detailed presentation of the results, which are organized by the major themes, or composite textural-structural descriptions, that emerged from the data during analysis. This chapter concludes with a summary of the findings.

Data Analysis

The video-recorded interviews were transcribed verbatim into Microsoft Word documents. The transcripts were imported as source files into NVivo 14 computer-assisted qualitative data analysis software. NVivo does not code the data. Instead, the software was used to maintain an auditable record of the decisions the researcher made during the data analysis process to enhance the dependability of the analysis. The following sections indicate how analysis methods were applied to the data in this study. In addition to the codes and themes, direct quotes from the participants are included below. Each quote is followed by a participant identifier to protect participants' privacy. For instance, P1 refers to the first participant, P2 the second participant, and so forth.

Step 1: Horizontalization

In the first step of the analysis, each transcript was broken down into meaning units (Moustakas, 1994). Each meaning unit was a quote or group of consecutive quotes that expressed a single meaning relevant to describing a participant's experience of Black motherhood. All the meaning units were then listed. During this step of the analysis, each of the meaning units was treated as equally relevant and significant; this was the meaning of "horizontalizing" the data. A total of 206 meaning units were identified and horizontalized from across the 10 transcripts.

Step 2: Data Reduction and Elimination

In this step, the meaning units were compared to one another. Redundant meaning units were eliminated, such that when two or more meaning units from a single participant described the same experience of Black motherhood, only the most complete description was retained for further analysis, and the less complete descriptions were eliminated from further analysis. Additionally, meaning units that did not include sufficient information to serve as a standalone description of a participant's experience when they were extracted from their context in the original transcript were eliminated. Meaning units that could not be summarized into a general, third-person description were also eliminated. After data reduction and elimination, 120 meaning units remained for further analysis. The meaning units that were eliminated from further analysis were retained in the original transcripts in case reconsideration of their relevance was needed.

Step 3: Identification of Invariant Constituents

The meaning units that were not redundant, that contained sufficient information to serve as standalone descriptions when extracted from their original contexts in the transcripts, and that could be summarized in a general, third-person description were identified as invariant constituents of the phenomenon of interest, which was Black motherhood, and how Black mothers navigate their fear of losing Black sons to death by racism. A total of 120 invariant constituents of the phenomenon were therefore identified across the 10 transcripts.

Step 4: Thematizing Invariant Constituents

The invariant constituents were thematized by clustering related invariant constituents. When new invariant constituent themes appeared in subsequent transcripts, they were applied as necessary. Table 2 indicates the 17 invariant constituent themes into which the 120 invariant constituents were clustered and which transcripts the themes were identified in.

Table 2

Invariant Constituent Themes (Initial Codes)

✓ = code identified in transcript

Invariant constituent theme (initial code)	P1	P2	P3	P4	P5	P6	P7	P8	P9	P10
Advocate for fairness and equality with authority figures			✓	✓	✓	✓				✓
Communication and awareness are key to protection	✓		✓		✓			✓		✓
Educating sons on how to navigate police encounters	✓	✓	✓	✓	✓	✓	✓	✓	✓	✓
Educating sons about racism and discrimination	✓	✓		✓			✓		✓	✓
Feel Law Enforcement officers are Untrustworthy	✓			✓		✓		✓	✓	✓
Faith in God	✓			✓		✓	✓	✓	✓	✓
Fostering awareness of culture and heritage					✓	✓		✓		
Identification with mother of victims of police brutality	✓	✓		✓	✓	✓	✓	✓	✓	✓
Law Enforcement were biased against Black males		✓	✓				✓		✓	✓
Negative stereotyping		✓	✓				✓			
Passing on values and teaching their sons to be proud Black males	✓		✓	✓	✓		✓	✓		✓
Police officer training needs to improve	✓					✓	✓	✓	✓	
Law Enforcement are perceived as threats to Black male children	✓	✓	✓	✓	✓					
Racial profiling is common	✓		✓	✓		✓		✓		
Serving as son's protector	✓	✓							✓	
Serving as son's role model						✓		✓	✓	
Teaching their children how to avoid confrontation to remain safe	✓	✓	✓	✓				✓		

Step 5: Validating Invariant Constituent Themes

The invariant constituent themes were validated by comparing them to the original transcripts to ensure that they accurately reflected patterns of meaning in the participants' original responses. All the invariant constituent themes (i.e., initial codes) passed this test.

Step 6: Developing Textural Descriptions

Textural descriptions were developed by listing the invariant constituent themes from each transcript that described what the participants had experienced, along with the direct quotes from the transcripts associated with those invariant constituent themes. The textural descriptions, therefore, included the invariant constituent theme labels that described what the participant had experienced, as well as the descriptions of the experiences in the participant's own words. Table 3 indicates which invariant constituent themes were designated as textural descriptions.

Table 3

Invariant Constituent Themes (Initial Codes) Designated as Textural Descriptions

1. Advocate for fairness and equality with authority figures
2. Communication and awareness are key to protection
3. Educating sons on how to navigate police encounters
4. Educating sons about racism and discrimination
5. Faith in God
6. Fear of sons being victimized
7. Feel Law Enforcement officers are untrustworthy
8. Fostering awareness of culture and heritage
9. Identification with mother of victims of police brutality
10. Passing on values and teaching sons to be proud Black males
11. Law Enforcement is perceived as threats to Black male children
12. Serving as son's protector
13. Serving as son's role model
14. Teaching their sons how to avoid confrontation to remain safe

Step 7: Developing Structural Descriptions

Structural descriptions were developed by listing the invariant constituent themes from each transcript that described the social, organizational, and other contexts of the experiences described in the individual textural descriptions, along with the direct quotes from the transcripts associated with those invariant constituent themes. Table 4 indicates which invariant constituent themes were designated as structural descriptions.

Table 4

Invariant Constituent Themes (Initial Codes) Designated as Structural Descriptions
1. Feel Law Enforcement officers are untrustworthy
2. Law Enforcement biased against Black males
3. Negative stereotyping
4. Police officer training needs to improve
5. Racial profiling is common

Step 8: Developing Composite Textural-Structural Descriptions

In the final step of the analysis, related textural and structural descriptions were clustered and combined across participants to identify overarching patterns of meaning in the data. The resulting composite textural-structural descriptions, or final themes, emerged as the major findings in this study. Table 5 indicates how the textural and structural descriptions were grouped to form the final themes.

Table 5

Grouping of Textural and Structural Descriptions into Final Composite Themes		
Composite Theme Textural and structural descriptions grouped to form theme	Participants contributing (N=10)	Meaning units assigned to theme

Theme 1: Benefits of raising a Black male child included passing on values and serving as a role model and protector	10	15
Passing on values and teaching their sons to be proud Black males	7	7
Serving as son's protector	3	3
Serving as son's role model	3	5
Theme 2: Racism had negative impacts on the experience of raising a Black male child	10	23
Feel Law Enforcement officers are untrustworthy	6	9
Fear of their sons being victimized	6	8
Negative stereotyping	3	6
Theme 3: Black mothers empower their Black male children against the impacts of racism	10	27
Advocate for fairness and equality with authority figures	5	7
Communication and awareness are key to protection	5	5
Educating sons about racism and discrimination	6	7
Fostering awareness of culture and heritage	3	3
Teaching sons to value and be proud of themselves	5	5
Theme 4: Law Enforcement was perceived as a threat to Black male children	10	33
Identification with mother of victims of police brutality	9	11
Law Enforcement biased against Black males	5	5
Police officer training needs to improve	5	7
Law Enforcement are perceived as threats to Black male children	5	5
Racial profiling is common	5	5
Theme 5: Black mothers navigated the fear of losing their sons through educating their sons and through reliance on faith	10	22
Educating sons on how to navigate police encounters	10	15
Faith in God	7	7

Themes

The research question was: How do Black mothers navigate their fears of potentially losing their sons during interactions with police officers? Five themes emerged during data analysis to indicate the participants' experiences of navigating those fears: (Theme 1) benefits of raising a Black male child included passing on values and serving as a role model and protector, (Theme 2) racism had negative impacts on the experience of raising a Black male child, (Theme 3) Black mothers empower their Black male children against the impacts of racism, (Theme 4) Law Enforcement was perceived as a threat to Black male children, and (Theme 5) Black mothers navigated the fear of losing their sons through educating their sons and through reliance on faith. The following sections are presentations of these themes.

Theme 1: Benefits of Raising a Black Male Child Included Passing on Values and Serving as a Role Model and Protector

All 10 participants contributed data to this theme. The participants indicated three experiences of benefits of raising their Black male children. They described experiences of passing on their values as one benefit, saying that as Black mothers, they felt responsible for passing on the values they had been raised with and that they wanted their sons to continue to uphold. Some participants also said that they experienced being their sons' protectors and role models.

Seven of the participants spoke of their experiences of passing on their values to their Black male children. P1 described passing on her family values as a benefit: *"I see the benefit as being able to raise a strong, courageous, respectable Black male and passing down family values of my ancestors that I've learned throughout my life. And just, you know, teaching them to overcome different challenges that they may face. I take pride in being able to show them kindness and love."*

P8 agreed, saying of the benefits of raising a Black male child, *"For me, it's to build a legacy, to carry our family traditions, carry on our family name, to show society what a Black man can be, and to show that we're not what the stereotype says."* P5 spoke of the benefit of being able to pass on a legacy inherited from strong, Black men:

> *I've been surrounded by very strong, loving, educated, and committed Black men, and so I think my strength in raising my sons comes from that. My father-in-law was a great man, my husband actually knew intimately both of his great-grandfathers. And so, the legacy that both of us have descended from gave us a great, firm foundation. It has grounded us, not only in a community aspect but a family aspect, and then the responsibility as an offspring to carry that forward, and so, being able to give that to my sons.*

Thus, the participants spoke of the benefits of raising their Black male children as including being able to pass down family values, traditions, names, and legacies inherited from the past, providing continuity for their families and heritage.

Three participants spoke of being their sons' protectors as a benefit of raising their Black male children. P1 described herself as a protector and teacher of her sons: *"I would consider motherhood to be very strong. I would say that I actively see myself as a protector, being able to have unconditional support and love, and always being able to be that teacher as we all are as parents. I consider myself to be their teacher."* P2 said of motherhood, *"of everything I went through in my life, being a mother has been the biggest blessing that I have."* Asked what she valued about motherhood, P2 explained, "*It's protectionism. I don't even know if that's a word, but it's a feeling of protecting them, no matter how old they get, if they're hurt.*" P9 spoke of having to protect her son from things that may lead to trouble:

> So, for me, it was about protection, making sure that he didn't get involved in things that could lead to him getting in trouble. Basically, you know, he never got to spend the night at anybody's house, and I was like, no, because what someone may do or think at their home may not be okay. So, I think sometimes it's a challenge because you try to be so over, so overprotective. It took a lot for me to allow him to experience things because there are so many things in life that you know can harm him. And so, I was so busy trying to protect him from things, keep him away from things.

Thus, protection could take the form of nurturance, as in P2's and P9's response.

Three of the participants said that they perceived themselves as their sons' role models. P9 said that she perceived her task as a mother as, "*empowering and equipping, and I understood that could only come if he saw it in me as well.*" P9 added that her role in teaching her son by example did not end when he became an adult: "*I had to make myself better in order to mother him better, and that still to this day, I mean, he's 30 years old now, with his own wife, and his own kids, and my idea with him is that I teach him that parenting never ends.*"

P6 spoke of how her journey to earn her master's degree despite the obstacles she needed to overcome as a Black woman and single mother was intended in part as an example to teach her son to overcome any obstacles that confronted him:

Being a mother raising a Black male child in this society in which we live, we cannot deny that it's racist. So, I'm finishing up my master's. I've experienced different racial things throughout my life. But once I stepped into higher education, I got to know people, you kind of find out just having to overcome just being looked at differently. I recognize that I had the same opportunity as others, but getting there and staying there was much more difficult for me, based on the support I was getting or the lack thereof. But still, having to overcome it. I'm entering my final semester. I'll be graduating this year. And so, looking back, I'm like, "Wow, you know, I did it, we're here". . . So, the fact that I have overcome, and I've been able to maintain a healthy heart and attitude toward even people who have done me unfairly, opens my mind to let my son know, "You can do it. You can do it because Mom was able to do it, and I'm raising you to be stronger than me."

P8 indicated in one of her responses how being a role model to a son could be a benefit to a mother: *"My strength is supporting my son and fighting for him, encouraging him in every way, any time."* P8 stated in this response that supporting her son and fighting for him gave her strength. It is reasonable to conclude that wanting to be a role model and set an example for their sons also gave participants such as P6 and P9 strength when they needed to overcome obstacles, as well. The participants needed their strength and resiliency, because racism raised several barriers in their lives and the lives of their Black male children, as the following theme indicates.

Theme 2: Racism Had Negative Impacts on the Experience of Raising a Black Male Child

All 10 participants contributed data to this theme. Most participants noted that they experienced living with fear of their Black male children being victimized by racist attacks on their ethnicity, dignity, opportunities, or physical safety. Most participants also perceived their sons living in a society that confronted them continually with racial bias and discrimination. Negative stereotyping was also a constant threat to Black male children, the participants said.

Six participants spoke of their experience of feeling that their sons lived in a society that viewed them as threats simply because of the color of their skin, thereby placing them under continual threat of attack or insult. P5 described the sense of vulnerability she felt in knowing that her sons, whom she experienced as parts of herself, might be attacked at any time:

> *Knowing that you have a heartbeat that exists and walks around outside of your body, and you are not able to control how people view your heartbeat—to know that when my sons got to a certain age, they were no longer considered young Black boys. They were men, or suspects, or subjects, or threats. As this has always been, this is where the devastating part comes in, that devastation of knowing that my incredibly smart, and talented, and loving, comedic human beings are not seen that way (as "incredibly smart, talented," etc., but rather as "threats or suspects)."*

In a second example of a Black mother's description of what it was like for her to worry constantly about her son's safety in a racist society, P1 mentioned unjustifiable police brutality as one of the threats her sons faced. She also emphasized the color of her sons' skin as the arbitrary, indelible marker that put them at risk of racist violence:

> One of the interview questions presented in this study was: What are the challenges in raising a Black male child? P1 response, the consistent worrying that's not the norm. I have to worry over and beyond the average because of the color of my children's skin tone. So, that's one thing that keeps me worrying all day long. It's worrying. Once they leave this house, and even in some cases when they're even in the house. I'm consistently worrying. I'm unable to provide the necessary protections that they may need. We can only do so much. And still, that feels like it's not enough. I am concerned about police brutality and discrimination. This is due to the color of their skin. Yes, totally due to the color of their skin.

P2's response is included here as one final example because she added a description of the significant effects of worrying about her son's safety on her mental health, citing anxiety, depression, and PTSD:

> I feel paranoid for my sons every time they leave the house, even if they're at work. I called. I tell them to text me to call me because I'm paranoid. I don't know if they're going to get stopped. They have licenses, they have insurance, they have jobs and everything. But I still worry about society in general because just going to work, they can get pulled over and killed on their way home. They can get pulled over assuming to be drug dealers. It is a possibility I will never see my sons again. So, it's affecting me because I feel paranoid. I have anxiety. I have depression. I have PTSD. I'm constantly worried whenever they're out of my sight.

These responses from P1, P2, and P5 were representative of the responses of other participants. They indicated the fear that the participants felt for their Black male children because of knowing the threat of racist violence under which their sons lived. Their navigation of this fear was the topic of this study, so the responses quoted here may bear some emphasis. It may be noted in P5's response that her sense of vulnerability associated with the threat to her sons felt to her as though the most intimate part and function of her body, her heart, and its beating, was walking around outside of her, out of her sight, and constantly at risk. It may be noted in P1's response that she felt such a sense of helplessness that she did not believe she could always protect her sons even when they were in her own home. P2 emphasized the catastrophic effects on her mental health of continually fearing for her sons' lives, which she called "paranoia." P2 did not consider her fears irrational; she said that no matter how legitimate her sons' activities and how irreproachable their conduct, *"they can get pulled over and killed on their way to work or on their way home"* for nothing more than, as P1 said, *"the color of their skin."* This was the lived experience of these mothers' fears: the continual potential for a catastrophic consequence for a completely arbitrary cause.

In addition to continually facing the threat of violence, the participants' sons continually faced racial bias and discrimination, which affected the participants as their mothers. P10 said of trying to prepare her son for the racial bias and discrimination he would inevitably face: *"I think that was a challenge to try to raise him to know that there are going to be people out there that will treat you differently because of the color of your skin."* P4 spoke of having to prepare her son to work twice as hard to achieve the same results as an individual from a dominant group

who did not have to struggle against discrimination:
> *We have to make sure that they [her sons] work twice as hard, doing things twice as better as other races, because they already look at us with disgust, or they are better than us. So, I have to make sure that he is not made to feel less than. I have to make sure that I stay on top of making sure he knows the difference between the two [feeling less than and being a victim of discrimination], because Black boys have to deal with a lot.*

P8 spoke sadly in saying, "*I just feel like, because of the color of his skin, the opportunities that others may get may be much more than what my son would get.*" Thus, the participants were saddened and dismayed; they remained motivated to teach and prepare their sons by their awareness of the obstacles that their sons faced in a society where systemic racism worked against them. Negative stereotyping was also a threat to their sons, some participants said, particularly because it could lead to racist violence or discrimination if their sons were stereotyped as threatening or criminals merely because of the color of their skin. P7 described the stereotypes that she said resulted in children of different races being treated differently by teachers in schools:

> *I've noticed the challenge for me is the stigma or the stereotype that you know little Black boys are bad. They're always troublesome, you know. They're dropouts: they're kind of Ghetto, or they're gonna be drug dealers. They don't know what they want to do in life. To me, the challenge I run into with my son is school because some people go by what society says about them {Black males}; they assume, too, that he's growing up in an environment where the mother may be on welfare, and she doesn't care about them. So, I find that the challenge for me is when he*

comes home and says the teacher ignored him or didn't give him a chance to speak. When he raises his hand, she's not allowing him to answer the question. My son noticed other kids, White kids in the class, are allowed to answer questions, and then when it comes to him, she ignores him. So, a lot of times, the challenge for me is going up to the school, speaking with the teacher, and talking to her face to face.*

P3 spoke of being conflicted, with part of her wanting to support her sons' right to express themselves freely in their clothing and hairstyles and another part of her wanting to advise her sons to dress and groom themselves in a more conservative, conventional way, to reduce the risk that they would be negatively stereotyped by law enforcement and other authority figures who could hurt them: *"I'm kind of torn, because I believe everybody has a right to express themselves through their clothing and hairstyles the way they want to, and at the same time, I know that these hairstyles many times are stereotyped, and people, businesses, and law enforcement automatically throw a label on our Black boys."*

P2 spoke more generally concerning stereotypes among Black boys and men. P2 indicated that a Black boy or man's skin color alone was sufficient to trigger racist stereotypes in people who held racist views: *"They see his skin color and automatically put the stereotype of anger, rage, violence, and drugs, all the negativity that they've always placed on Black men before they even get to know them."* Given that the threats of violence, discrimination, and stereotyping were so pervasive, the participants reported that they oppose the effects of racism on their Black male children, as the following theme indicates.

Theme 3: Black Mothers Empower Their Black Male Children Against the Impacts of Racism

All 10 participants contributed data to this theme. Participants expressed that communication and awareness-raising about racism and its effects were key to protecting their Black male children. Accordingly, the participants engaged in educating their sons about racism, often from a very young age. The participants also reported that they engaged in advocating for their sons with authority figures and teaching their sons to value themselves, as well as in fostering in their sons an awareness of their culture and heritage.

The participants described communication and awareness-raising with their sons as key to protecting them. P10 expressed this perception by stating, *"I'm protecting him by just speaking the truth and telling him to be cautious."* P1 agreed, saying, *"Communication is awareness . . . I allow openness to have tough conversations about situations concerning racism that they may or may not come across. Communication is key with my boys."* P8 also said, *"I try to be open and honest with him. I just believe in being real with my son, not pretending, not faking, or lying . . . So that was my main thing of trying to protect him."*

One of the topics about which the participants communicated openly and honestly with their sons was racism. P9 said that she began to teach her son about racism when he was *"Probably around 10 or 11."* P9 stated, *"I definitely educated him about racism . . . I said simply that there are some people that are going to treat you wrong just because you're Black. For no reason. You haven't opened your mouth and said anything. You haven't done anything."* P10 said, *"I think I can go back to when he was about 4 or 5. He didn't really understand, but I taught *him at a young age to always be respectable, and everybody's not gonna like him because of the color of his skin. I elaborated on that with my son all the time."* P7 said of how she began to teach her son about racism, *"When he was maybe in the third or fourth grade, I remember saying to my son you're gonna find that some people won't like you based on the color of your skin, and you may be judged. But that's a part of life."* P1 said that she had to start teaching her young sons about racism at an early age when children of other races refused to play with them:

> *In educating young Black males, it has to start at a very early age. I know, for me with my sons, it started very early on. From when they were in elementary school, we lived in a predominantly White neighborhood, and they went to a school that was mostly all White, and there were cases where other kids didn't want to play with them because they are Black. They don't want to be close to them or touch them because they thought something was wrong with them, because they have darker skin. So, I have to explain to my children when they come home. Why didn't this person want to play with them? So, from early on, I've had to teach my sons that they are different; although they are not different, they are human beings, too. Their skin color is different, and they will be treated differently just solely based on that fact.*

Thus, the participants' teachings to their sons about racism typically began at a young age and involved preparing their sons for rejection and discrimination, and also involved preparing their sons to understand that rejection and discrimination as both inevitable ("a part of life," P7) and arbitrary ("for no reason," P9).

Five participants indicated that part of protecting their

Black male children was advocating for fairness and equality for their sons. P5 said that she advocated for her sons with teachers to allow her sons to have the freedom to be themselves: *"When my boys were going through school, I advocate for them more to just be children, and that if my children can't just be children in your classroom, then they need another classroom."* P7 also spoke of advocating for her son's teachers to provide him with the same attention as other children and treat him with fairness and care in class:

> *So, she's not really helping {the teacher}. And so, this is just another troubled Black kid in my class, so I'm gonna treat him a certain way. But then this challenges me to go to the school and say, hey, wait a minute. You're not treating my child fairly. I need to let you know that I am a very active parent, and I'm in his life full time, and if there are some issues or concerns. Don't take it out on him, you know. You can discuss it with me. You know. I've had issues where they've yelled at him, and then the teacher actually looked at my son who is Black, and then other Black kids, you know, basically pointing them out as Blacks, you know, emphasizing that. So, things like that. And then I had to basically confront the teacher in front of the principal and the vice principal. Letting them know that, even though he's a Black child, you didn't have to treat him that way.*

P4 was also a strong advocate for her son with schools: *"I spoke with teachers, superintendents. I wrote letters. I am an advocate for my son because he doesn't know how to express himself, and I had to let them know that my son is being mistreated."* It may be noted in these participants responses that they appeared to feel that it was necessary for them to be strong advocates for their sons just to obtain for them the same consideration that other students received as a matter of course, as when P7 needed to meet with her son's teachers to have the same consideration shown to her son as was shown to *"another kid in the class, and in this case ideally other White kid."*

Five participants spoke of teaching their sons to be proud of who they are as an urgent priority and part of their roles as Black mothers. P1 said that she worked to ensure for her sons *"That they understand that they are equal, and they are just as good as anyone else, to make them understand that they are just as good as anyone else, no matter what color they are."* P2 perceived it as a challenge to overcome the negative stereotypes that are imposed on her sons and defeat them with more positive messages:

> *I believe Black is beautiful. To have a Black child is the biggest honor for me. Our Black males are so underrated, and they've been persecuted so much. But I try to make sure that I tell all my sons that you are somebody. You are a king. That's the crown you hold. They're strong, they're beautiful, even though society doesn't always treat them that way. I try to always make sure that they know that you are somebody.*

P8 said that she told her son, *"In Junior High I really started to drill it in his head that there are people that may hate you because of the color of your skin . . . But be true to yourself. Don't let anyone discourage you; always remember you are somebody."* Thus, these participants recognized that their sons faced racially discriminatory obstacles, and they worked to counteract those obstacles by explicitly teaching their sons at all costs to value themselves and be proud of who they are.

Three participants said that part of protecting their Black

male children involved teaching them their history and heritage. P5 spoke of teaching her sons about their Black history and culture:

> *I recall that our family discussions around our ethnicity, our culture, our heritage, really centered around our strengths and our accomplishments. I used to have a lot of summer homework assignments for my children to keep them engaged, and I home-schooled as well. Throughout the years of them growing up, a lot of our projects were around making sure that they knew more about Black leaders, activists, poets, politicians, actors, and, you know, activists like Martin Luther King, Harriet Tubman, and Malcolm X, and if they had an interest in a particular person, like a Martin Luther King, or Dr. King, or Malcolm X, then they learn more. Right. And yeah, so we've had a lot of those conversations.*

P6 reported that she was dissatisfied with her son for the lack of exposure to Black history in schools:

> *So, this was actually pretty recent this year in Black History month. It is the first time where I recognize they didn't spend much time in school on it, you know. I remember just asking him {her son}, you know what are you guys learning in school, are you learning about Black history? I felt like you're not learning enough. Last year, we went to the African Diaspora Museum in San Francisco. There, they sell books for children on young Black women and Black men pioneers, so there's also pictures and a short paragraph on their life. You know, I pull the books out, and you know, read them to him, it touched on slavery a little bit. I just told him. There was a time where Black people and White people couldn't live*

> in the same place, and even to the point where sometimes Black people were slaves, you know. They weren't treated nicely, you know, and such like that. So this was the first year where I kinda did go in a little bit because I realized he's in his developing years, and if he was not learning about Black history, now we need to start. So yeah.

Theme 4: Law Enforcement Perceived as a Threat to Black Male Children

All 10 participants contributed data to this theme. Participants indicated that they perceived police officers as threats to their Black male children. One of the reasons for this is that each participant's perception comes from either a personal experience with law enforcement or from the media showing unarmed African Americans being killed by law enforcement. The participants felt as mothers that they could identify with the mothers who lost their sons to police brutality and murder; they reported because they perceived that their sons could be victims of similar violence.

The participants reported trust in law enforcement has either decreased due to past experiences or they have never trusted law enforcement due to the ongoing violence of Black Americans. P1 shares an encounter with a police officer while taking her sons to school:

> *I was taking my kids to school, and a couple of their buddies had spent the night, so I was taking them all to school very early in the morning, and I was pulled over by a White officer. I was a bit puzzled because I didn't understand what the problem was. He first told me that my license was not up to date and made me get out of the car in front of all the kids. I pointed out to him that my*

license was indeed up to date. He then told me I had a broken taillight. The fact of the matter is that wasn't the issue, either. I was profiled because I was a Black woman with four teenage Black boys in my car.

P5 explains her experience with a police encounter; despite being the person coming to help resolve a contentious matter, she was put in handcuffs and put in the back of a police car:

> There was a dispute at my family home, and I remember I was coming home from work, and my family member called me needing help to manage a situation. It wasn't anything too bad, but the police were called by a neighbor. They arrived soon after I got there. I got out of my car and started walking towards the house. I immediately got taken into handcuffs. The White woman, who actually was the one who was at the time drunk and causing the disturbance, got to sit down on the ground. I got sat in the back of a police car. That was my first time ever getting sat in the back of a police car, and I had nothing to do with the situation at all. And I'm like, Okay, I was scared. Cause I'm like, I did nothing, you know. So yeah, that was my first encounter.

P2 shares that she was pulled over by a police officer for being in the wrong neighborhood:

> I was stopped by a police officer. And he said I didn't make a complete stop. First of all, I seen him behind me. So, I knew I made a complete stop. He said {police officer} why am I in this area, which is a predominantly White area. I said I didn't know it was against the law to drive out here, and he said where do I live. When he looked at my license. Well, you live in another city. Why are you here?

> And I told him I was taking my daughter-in-law to work. He said can I search your car. I said no, I know my rights. And then it was like, you can go; we're not gonna give you a ticket.

Several participants were direct in expressing their views of why they lost confidence in the police, and they feel law enforcement is untrustworthy and are perceived as threats.

The participants reported that they perceived law enforcement as threats to Black male children; P5 framed this perception from a historical perspective:

> And there is not a great relationship between law enforcement and my community, while I can appreciate what the job description entails: service and protection. I also believe that law enforcement is much heavier on enforcement, and I do believe that, unfortunately, it is a system like all others. It is a part of an oppressive system that has its foundation in policing Black people and our communities, I mean. Law enforcement was created to keep Black folks enslaved. Do I think that every law enforcement agency or police officer is inherently racist? No. Do I agree that they are trained and shaped by a racist system? Absolutely.

P1 spoke of feeling saddened by the sense that police officers, who claim to be protectors for her culture, were, in fact, she feels some officers are enemies to her community: *"I don't feel too good about police officers, and it saddens me to say that because they are supposed to be our protectors, and instead of looking at a police officer as a protector, it's almost like a sense of seeing them more so as enemies, not toward everyone, but toward my culture."*

P2 had worked closely with police officers in her job, and

she spoke from extensive experience in saying:
> *For some of them {police officers}, I feel like they are trying to make a difference. But considering I've worked as special police for several years, to me, they're KKK with a badge, to be honest. I've seen it on both spectrums with my children as well as working behind the scenes. For example, when we were working on the transit, 98% of the tickets given were to Black people. I feel that the police overreacted several times with Black people. I've seen the harassment of the Black people just like the tickets; they run their names. They're handcuffing them, detaining them, and it was something different for every Black person they stopped. So, I made sure that you know I spoke up for them because they couldn't speak up for themselves at that time.*

P4 said simply, "*There are those bad apples that make the whole department look bad. They're supposed to protect and serve, and they actually take their power, and they misuse it.*"

Participants perceived law enforcement as threats to their sons in part because they perceived law enforcement has demonstrated unwarranted, excessive, unjustifiably, and often illegal use of force in many of its encounters with Black males. P9 referred to news stories of Black children being placed in potentially choke holds for being in community pools:
> *This is my truth. I assume that most police officers are racist. I think that because, like, you know, when I see young Black boys and girls being choked by police officers because somebody didn't want them at a community pool. I'm like, you can't do that; you have no regard for these young people as human beings, as somebody that you're supposed to be protecting.*

P10 shared that she feels that police are more likely to use force against Black males then their White counterparts because some police feel Black men are threats, a consequence of racist stereotyping, about which she had warned her son:

> *I feel that police officers need to interact more with people of color, because, like I said, they have in their mindset that they're doing the right thing. I think it's their upbringing that brings them to this attitude that Black men should be feared. You know, I think that most police officers are afraid of the unknown. People fear the unknown when they have a different perspective of you. So, they're harsher towards people of color. I think. I mean, we've seen that on TV, you know, all the murders and assaults on Black men that interacted with police officers, and I make sure my son is aware of that. And that's why we tell him to be submissive.*

The participants identified with the mothers whose sons were victims of police brutality and murder whose stories were well publicized in the media. P9 expressed her pain over two young Black boys 12 and 14 who were murdered by police officers and how she saw her son in these two young boys:

> *Tamir Rice really hit home for me because I saw my son in him. I'm gonna be honest, it made me fearful. I definitely felt the disregard for a young man that was killed in Missouri by an officer. Michael Brown was his name, but you know, he was shot in the middle of the street. I mean, again, no regard for these young boys' lives; nothing even warrants that. My heart breaks for the mothers. And I was thinking that could've so easily been him {her son}.*

P7 spoke about shootings of unarmed African Americans and the related media coverage, and she shared the hurt she felt for the parents and families of the young males' murder by police officers, particularly she felt the need to educate her son about the victims:

> *It just really made me sad. It made me feel like. you know, hurt for the parents and all the families of these young males, or you know, what they had to go through. And yes, I saw it on TV, and it made me feel like I had to make a difference. I needed to educate my son about it and how you know in society this is really what's happening, but I don't know how to shield him. I just try to educate him and let him know that this happens in the world and that not all police officers are that way.*

P7 continued to express her reaction to a young man who was pulled over by a police officer:

> *But I do get emotional when I see it happening on television and social media. You know, it hit close to home for me because it was a young man that was recently in the media that was from Sacramento that, you know, got pulled over, and they didn't even give him an explanation as to why they were pulling them over. And you know, he ended up being scared and ran off, and they ended up killing him. But that, to me, really hurts.*

P1 spoke of the fear she felt when she identified two nationally recognized victims of racist violence killed and thought this could be her own son's reality:

> *Trayvon Martin, that hit home with me because he was just a young boy who had so much life ahead of him; he was just walking with his hood on. And if you see most of these kids today, their clothing is baggy clothes and hoodies. They all have cell phones. So, the thought that my sons could be just walking with a hoodie on and could*

> be killed by the police scares me. Yes, the Trayvon Martin story hit home, also George Floyd; those two situations hit home really badly.

P4 reflected on her own experience of the heartbreaking feeling of having a Black son and watching video of the suffocating George Floyd calling out for his mother: *"The one that stuck out to me was George Floyd. That was very impactful to me because I have a Black son, and the first thing that any Black boy or man will do is call for his mama."* P4 said that she imagined how she would have felt if it were her son in the video: *"When he called out for his mother, every mother had to feel the same thing, knowing if that was their son lying there with someone's knee on their neck and watching the breath go out of them."* Participants feel law enforcement officers were improperly trained. The question was asked to each participant: If you could talk to a police captain or police officer what might you tell them? P1 had this to say: *"I think that I will ask them {police officers}, Why did you get into this line of work? Did you get into this line of work to help everybody, to make sure that everyone is safe? No matter age, color, race, language, or was it solely for personal alternative motives."* P9 shared her concerns relating to citizens and their communities:

> In terms of the police interactions, I would say. I think it's really important on every level that they have to know the people you are servicing in the communities that you're addressing. Not just what you observed. But being able to communicate with a population in terms of what's important to them. What are their fears? What are their desires for their community? What are they seeing in their community? You know. How do they feel police either adds to their community or negatively impacts it?

P6 also shared her thoughts:
> *It is so important that whatever way your new police officers or current police officers are taught, you know. Revisit the curriculum, revisit the training. Things have to change. The population has to change. Culture has to change, acceptance and tolerance have to change, but there still remains that remnant of racial discrimination and issues between the police academy, police officers, and Black people. So, my question, what are you guys doing to make sure that we don't continue with this trend because it's been steady, it hasn't let up. So, it needs to change, you know, so that would be my main thing.*

The following theme indicates how the participants navigated the fear they felt in knowing that, at any time, their sons could be victims of racist brutality by the hands of police officers.

Theme 5: Black Mothers Navigated the Fear of Losing Their Sons Through Educating Their Sons and Through Reliance on Faith

All 10 participants contributed data to this theme. The participants indicated that one of the primary ways they navigated their fear of potentially losing their sons to police violence was by educating their sons about how to be safe during encounters with police (e.g., staying calm, submissive, and cooperative, keeping hands visible at all times, etc.). Educating their sons was the active role that the participants were able to take in keeping their sons safe if there were a potential encounter with law enforcement. The participants also indicated that they relied on their faith, spirituality, and their belief that God could or would keep their sons safe. Faith and spirituality reflected the participants' awareness of the limitations of their power to keep their sons safe.

All the participants reported that they educated their sons about how to stay alive during encounters with law enforcement. Providing this education was an active role that the participants were able to take as mothers in keeping their sons safe from police violence. P5 said that the overarching lesson she had tried to teach her sons was, "*When you get pulled over by a police officer when you have to interact with a police officer for any reason, remember your job is to get home safe and alive; we can defend your honor and your character later.*" P1 gave her sons detailed instructions on how to be safe during traffic stops:

> *Both my children drive, so … I have to continually educate them on what to do and what not to do if they're pulled over by a police officer. And so, I tell them to just be quiet and do what they say, and make sure that you always have your registration and ID on you. Beyond that, I remind them to put your hands up. Don't talk back, don't make a move. I have to engage in conversations with them to make sure they're not killed, versus just getting a ticket.*

P3 instructed her son to always be cooperative with law enforcement, no matter how unreasonable the officers' demands appeared to be:

> *We talked about it, how to be safe, to do what they tell him to do, even though it's very hard to tell your kid to let them yell at you or yell directions at you, and they still have to bite their tongues and do it. I think as a Black mother having Black sons, we have to get them to understand, to have talks with them about interactions with law enforcement.*

It may be noted that P3's instructions to her son appeared to echo P5's directive ("Your job is to get home. We can defend your honor and your character later"). P2 instructed her sons to always record any interactions with police during a traffic stop, and always to call her, no matter what time of day or night so that there would be a recording of the interaction and a witness:

> *As soon as they see the police lights turn on, call me Facetime. Don't make any sudden moves. Keep their phone where they can immediately use it before they [the police] even walk up to the window. Don't panic; make sure you have your license, and when they ask for it, hand it to them. Keep me on the phone with you. Facetime live, record it so we'll have a recording of it. And I just told them, make sure that's the first thing you do before they get out of the car and see any movement. Call me. I don't care if it's 3 o'clock in the morning so we can record the interactions with them from the time they say, "license and registration" to the end.*

P4 said that she started teaching simple lessons to her son when he was young: *"Never run. Always be compliant and know your rights."* P8 framed her advice to her son in simple terms: *"If you get pulled over, comply with their orders so that you can live."* Thus, the active role that the participants were able to take in keeping their sons safe was educating them about how to stay alive during encounters with law enforcement. By teaching them to be as compliant as possible, increasing the odds that their male Black children would make it home alive.

However, the participants recognized that because of the nature of arbitrary, racist violence, no amount of education they provided to their sons, and no amount of compliance on the part of their sons could entirely eliminate the possibility that their sons would be victimized. The participants, therefore, recognized the limitations in their ability to protect their sons and the limitations in their sons' ability to protect themselves. To cope with the fear associated with the resulting sense of powerlessness, most of the participants relied on religious faith. P9, for example, said, *"I realized that I could not continue long-term with worry, because worry, it will manifest itself in other ways, physically high blood pressure, headache, things like that. So, for me, I had to really lean on my faith."* P6 also spoke of coping with powerlessness through prayer: *"If I knew my child was with a police officer, I would be in serious prayer, because I know I can't do anything on my own."* P7 stated that her faith kept her from having to fear for her son continually:

> *I wonder on a daily basis when he leaves, "Oh, my gosh! I hope he doesn't run into a police officer, or he's gonna be maybe killed, or, you know, brutally beaten up." I don't do that on a daily basis because when I pray for my kids, I guess I just have a sense of peace that he's watched over through just putting my trust and faith in God. God will watch over him and protect him.*

P1 also said that she navigated her fear through prayer: *"I fear losing my sons to the hands of a police officer every time they leave out the door. The only way I know how to navigate this fear is through prayer."* P4 stated that her faith kept her from fear: *"I do not fear because my son is covered by the blood of the Lamb. I pray over him daily."* P8 also spoke of her prayer as a kind of shield for her son: *"How do I navigate it? With prayer . . . I pray for his safety and protection. Every day, I cover him with His blood, so that God will shield him from harm and danger, so that I don't worry."* Thus, the participants coped with their sense of powerlessness through religious faith and through their spiritual belief that through their prayer, they could call upon a higher power, which is God, to protect their sons.

Summary

Five themes emerged from the data to illustrate the lived experiences of Black mothers navigating their fears of possibly losing their sons during interactions with police officers: (1) the benefits of raising a Black male child included passing on values and serving as a role model and protector, (2) racism had negative impacts on the experience of raising a Black male child, (3) Black mothers opposed the impacts of racism on their Black male children, (4) law enforcement was perceived as a threat to Black male children, and (5) Black mothers empower their Black male children against the impacts of racism, as well as through reliance on faith. The data analysis indicated that these themes were interconnected in such a way that participants experienced significant fear about the possibility of their sons falling victim to police brutality. This fear significantly impacted their emotional well-being, parenting approaches, and mental health. Additionally, the mothers employed coping strategies such as resilience and faith as sources of strength and support. The mothers' experiential knowledge served as the foundation for the preliminary findings. The knowledge received was influenced by information obtained from lived experiences, historical racism, family, and media occurrences. The strategies that emerged among participants were focused on navigating fear and preparing their sons for potential police interactions. Next, we will move to Chapter Five, which includes discussion, interpretations, recommendations, limitations, and implications for future research based on these themes.

Chapter V

Discussion

The objective of this qualitative phenomenological study was to examine the lived experiences of how Black mothers navigate their fear of losing their sons during interactions with law enforcement. Additionally, the research sought to contribute to the existing literature on challenges that Black mothers encounter while safeguarding and raising their sons in a racist society, and the results of this study pave the way for additional and future research studies. The brutal treatment of African Americans by the United States of America began with the institution of slavery in the 16th century and has persisted to this day. Although there has been progressive progress in the fight for freedom, the long-standing effects of intergenerational trauma have had a significant impact on the mental well-being of many African Americans (Adedoyin et al., 2019). African American men have been unjustly vilified and exposed to recurrent acts of violence, humiliation, and homicide. The public has been significantly influenced by years of racist conditioning, resulting in the perception of African American men as a significant threat to public safety.

Consequently, law enforcement agents have been conditioned to treat them accordingly. The disproportionately high rates of police brutality directed toward African American males foster a culture of justified distrust toward law enforcement within the African American community (Adedoyin et al., 2019).

In addition, the extent of African American mothers' fear and lack of trust in the police has been significantly understated. Many African American men have been unjustifiably targeted as adversaries over the course of American history. Moreover, the experiences and challenges faced by African American mothers have consistently been downplayed and left unspoken (Jacobs, 2017).

The purpose of this research was to provide the Black mothers of this study with a forum to discuss their experiences and lend their voices to the question of how they navigate the possibility of losing their sons during interactions with police officers. Data was gathered from a sample of 10 participants using one-on-one video-recorded interviews. The interviews primarily consisted of open-ended questions. The interviews were transcribed and subsequently analyzed for similarities; the similarities were categorized and assigned codes. Meaning emerged from the codes, and themes were deduced. Following the notation of the initial themes, a total of five significant themes were identified. The participants' lived experiences were summarized using the following five themes that emerged from the data: benefits of raising a Black male child included passing on values and serving as a role model and protector; racism had negative impacts on the experience of raising a Black male child, Black mothers empower their Black male children against the impacts of racism, law enforcement was perceived as a threat to Black male children, and Black mothers navigated the fear of losing their sons through educating their sons and through reliance on faith.

The findings of this study demonstrate that Black mothers see themselves as protectors and role models for their sons and are responsible for instilling cultural and social values.

Participants reported effectively instilling positive morals and values in their sons by transmitting family values, traditions, and legacies inherited from previous generations. This approach helps their sons develop an appreciation and respect for their culture and themselves. In their efforts to empower and protect male children, the participants emphasized the significance of awareness-raising and effective communication. "The Talk" refers to a specific form of racial socialization in which many Black parents educate their children on how to conduct themselves safely and appropriately especially when interacting with law enforcement and other authoritative figures (Anderson et al., 2022). The participants also reported that their confidence in law enforcement has diminished either because of previous racial encounters or because they have never had trust in law enforcement due to the persistent violence against Black Americans. The results from this study indicate that the participants navigate their fear of potentially losing their sons due to the police's excessive use of force by engaging in education, raising awareness, utilizing effective communication, and relying on faith. These findings were both insightful and distressing. The Black mothers who participated in this study reported an experience of constant fear for the safety and well-being of their sons, regardless of their age. This fear exists even though most participants stated that their sons had not been directly involved in or encountered incidents of police violence. Due to widely publicized media coverage of instances of local and state police brutality involving unarmed African American males, Black mothers are subjected to ongoing psychological trauma. The findings corroborate the assertions made by Galovski et al. (2016) that African American mothers are not preoccupied with a few isolated incidents of violence but rather are impacted by more significant and systemic experiences of psychological trauma existing over several decades. Despite the challenges they faced raising their kids in a racist society, the Black mothers in this study persevere in their efforts to protect and empower their sons, relying on their resilience and faith. The participants acknowledged "GOD" as their main source of strength.

Self as a Researcher

I am a Black mother of eight beautiful children, four biological and four stepchildren, including five sons and three daughters. As a researcher, I chose this topic to research for several reasons. First, I believe it is imperative to give a voice to Black women, and in this case, I felt it was essential to give a voice to Black mothers who fear potentially losing their sons to police racial bias and brutality. Second, it was important to me because, as a Black mother whose son was victimized by police racial bias, law enforcement silenced my voice when I tried to speak up against the unfair treatment that my son received from a police officer. Unfair treatment was experienced by my son when he was targeted for an offensive term, "Driving While Black" (DWB). Racial profiling or racially motivated traffic stops conducted by law enforcement are commonly referred to as DWB (Lundman & Kaufman, 2003). According to Harris (2002), there is a prevailing belief that Black individuals, particularly in comparison to White individuals, are more susceptible to police scrutiny while driving a vehicle, primarily due to the color of their skin. The unethical treatment my son experienced in an interaction with a police officer resulted in him being transported to the hospital. A routine drive home from work turned into a nightmare. During the stop, according to my son, the police officer terrorized him with a police dog, warning him that the dog would attack him if he attempted to move. The officer placed him in the back seat of the police car with the air conditioning off. Several minutes later, after the officer rummaged through his belongings in his car, the police officer put the police dog in the back seat with my son, and the dog attacked him, biting him on his arm, leg, and face. The only way that I knew my son had been attacked was that a family friend was at the hospital when my son arrived, and they called me. It was a little over an hour before I could see my son. My son's Blood Alcohol Content was 0.0. It was a day that I will never forget seeing my child lying in a hospital bed, mauled by a police dog. Nothing happened to the police officers. As the mother of five Black sons and the grandmother of seven grandsons, I consistently harbor concerns about the potential for my children and grandchildren to encounter unethical and racist police officers in a negative manner. From the standpoint of an African American mother, it is deeply distressing to live in a society where I am constantly aware that my sons and the sons of other African American mothers may be subjected to harsh and unjust treatment by law enforcement purely due to their skin color. This is particularly troubling because police officers occupy a role in which society places the expectation that they will "protect and serve" all citizens equally. The compounding factor of this unsettling tendency is in the acknowledgment that a significant proportion of homicides involving innocent or unarmed African Americans typically do not result in a "guilty" verdict for law enforcement officials who perpetrate these horrendous and unwarranted offenses. This phenomenon can be attributed to systemic racism, which has historically seen African Americans as being presumed guilty until proven innocent (Chaney & Robertson, 2015, p. 64). Unfortunately, for most victims and their families, even after establishing innocence, the lives of the wrongfully killed innocent individuals cannot be restored, and apologies, regardless of their genuineness, are insufficient. Without conducting this research, my story, like that of several other Black mothers, would have remained untold. The participants' bravery in sharing their stories deeply moved me. I was captivated by the personal experiences of each participant as well as grateful to share this opportunity with them. It was personally significant for me to have the chance to listen attentively to their detailed accounts of what it was like for them to feel the fear of possibly losing their son to police violence, the challenges of protecting them from racism, and the benefits of raising Black male children. I related to their cultural experiences as a Black mother. I was able to reflect on their experiences honestly, respectfully, and sensitively. I thought a lot about the participants' powerful and deeply ingrained cultural beliefs and values, which shaped who they are as Black women, and how essential it was to them that their sons inherit those beliefs and values. Because I was able to identify and understand the participants' fears, anxiety, and challenges, I realized I needed to be aware of any biases and preconceptions. Since I had shared similar direct or indirect experiences, hearing the participants' personal experiences evoked a range of emotions in me. I utilized the epoch technique to deliberately set aside and remove any biases, preconceived ideas, and preconceptions. I accomplished this by documenting my emotions either by journal or field notes to increase my self-awareness and to monitor my preconceptions and tendency to be judgmental. This allowed me to shift my perspective and align myself with the participants, enabling me to understand their points of view while also recognizing my own biases. I ensured that I took these appropriate measures to preserve my emotions and retain a sense of protectiveness for the participants. This enabled me to approach their phenomenon objectively as if experiencing it for the first time (Moustakas, 1994). Each participant acknowledged their appreciation for the chance to use their voices to share their experiences because they were also aware of the significance of this research. I anticipated that this research would provide significant findings that will capture the interest of law enforcement agencies, legislators, marriage and family therapists, and other professionals involved in addressing the enduring disparities and injustices faced by African Americans and other individuals belonging to racial and ethnic minority groups. I desire that the mothers who participated in this study benefited tremendously psychologically and emotionally by allowing their voices to be heard, and other Black mothers will learn from this research how to navigate through their fear of potentially losing their sons to police racial bias and brutality.

Summary of the Findings

The research question developed to guide this study was: How do Black mothers navigate their fears of potentially losing their sons during interactions with police officers? Overall, five themes emerged during data analysis to indicate the participants' experiences of navigating those fears. For example, participants described the benefits of raising a Black male child, which included passing on their personal values and serving as a role model and protector. However, the perils of raising a Black male child were also discussed. Participants described the negative impacts of racism on the experience of raising a Black male child. Namely, the fear that their children would have their autonomy, physical safety, and/or life opportunities threatened was a real and persistent threat. To empower the impacts of racism, participants stated they used education, advocacy, and cultural pride to instill a sense of courage and self-esteem in their children. In addition to combating racism through empowerment, these practices also mitigated the threat presented by law enforcement, as well as the thought that their sons could potentially become victims of police violence. Finally, participants described navigating the fear of losing their sons through persistent, active education and through reliance on personal spirituality and faith.

Interpretation of the Findings

The discussion of the results is arranged based on the identified themes.

Theme 1: Benefits of Raising a Black Male Child Included Passing on Values and Serving as a Role Model and Protector

The results of this study indicated that Black mothers have the responsibility to raise their sons with the right social and cultural values. The participants see themselves as not only protectors but also role models for their sons. Because the police presence in the Black community has elicited feelings of fear and mistrust among the Black community, this is a prime reason the participants have become protective of their sons. Bailey et al. (2021) noted that Black male youths are twice as likely to be killed by police before the age of 21 than their White counterparts. The increased police violence among Black male youths increases the risk of death or injury during police encounters. Therefore, the participants feel the need to prepare their sons for potential police encounters. According to Black mothers in the current study, it is important to prepare their male children to be strong, courageous, and respectable so that they can overcome different challenges they may face in life, including police brutality. As reported in this study, the participants cultivate positive morals and values in their Black male children by passing down family values, traditions, and legacies inherited from the past is an effective strategy to instill in their sons to appreciate and cherish their culture and themselves.

As the current study established, participants also perceive themselves as their sons' role models. Black mothers empower and equip their sons with the knowledge and values necessary to thrive in a dominant culture. Hughes et al. (2006) state that ethnic-racial socialization processes can transmit knowledge about ethnicity and race. Using egalitarianism, Black mothers can encourage their sons to value their unique qualities and help them acquire the skills needed to thrive in a dominant culture (Hughes et al., 2006). With cultural socialization, the aim is to instill in children a sense of ethnic pride. Preparation for bias and using mistrust messages is essentially providing male children with strategies to be conscious, cautious and cope with racial discrimination (Hughes et al., 2006). According to Shah (2020), Black mothers use preparation for bias when engaging their sons to equip them with the values and ability to handle police encounters.

Theme 2: Racism Had Negative Impacts on the Experience of Raising a Black Male Child

Participants perceive their sons to be living in a society that strongly represents racial discrimination. Negative stereotyping is a threat to Black male children. The stereotype of young Black men as dangerous or threatening can have serious consequences for interactions with law enforcement. Black male children are viewed as threats because of the color of their skin and, in some incidents, physical stature, thereby placing them under continual threat of attack or insult. The participants reported constant worry about the safety of their sons because their sons' skin is an arbitrary, indelible marker that puts them at risk of racist violence.

The participants' stories confirmed that Black mothers feel the fear for their male children because of knowing the threat of racist violence under which their sons live is one of the challenges of raising a Black child in the U.S. Leath et al. (2020) stated that Black males are likely to experience violence because of the narratives and distorted images imposed on Black people, which has resulted in their portrayal as criminals, angry, and violent. In the social and cultural imaging of discriminatory law enforcement, Black men's perceived violence and criminality and the accompanying narrative, such as resisting arrest and breaking the law, are always used as an excuse to cause harm. The demonizing and disfiguring narratives and images have played a key role in marginalizing the lives of Black male children. Due to racism, Black people are seen as lesser and inferior human beings, making it easier to justify any action taken against them.

Theme 3: Black mothers empower their Black male children against the impacts of racism

To empower and protect Black male children from racism, the participants cited the importance of communication and raising awareness. The participants educate their children about racism and its impact often from a young age. Education revolves around increasing the value of Black male children and their cultural awareness. By understanding the history, contributions, and achievements of their forefathers, the participants instill a sense of pride and belonging in their children. Mothers can explain how physical and psychological resilience a cornerstone of the history of African Americans has been, showcasing the

the perseverance and strengths of people who faced and conquered racism and adversity. Fostering children's awareness of their culture and heritage is an effective way of improving their ability to understand how to overcome racial discrimination.

The current study's findings are consistent with existing literature. For example, Turner (2020) suggested that by supporting Black male children's sense of individuality, Black mothers help nurture their self-esteem. The process includes educating them to champion their self-concepts, self-expression, interests, and talents regardless of whether these elements conform or diverge from societal expectations or family norms or not. Similarly, Powell and Coles (2021) highlighted that setting achievable goals is an effective way for Black mothers to build their sons' self-awareness. Parents work in collaboration with their children to identify realistic goals in different areas, including academics, hobbies, sports, and other individual development areas such as personality, emotions, beliefs, and values. Celebrating these achievements, however small or large, improves the child's trust in their capabilities regardless of other people's opinions.

Participants in this study noted that to protect their sons from police encounters, they start to teach their sons about racism early on in life. The participants teach their Black sons to understand that some people will treat them differently simply because of their skin color. When it comes to educating their sons on racism, communication is the key. Utilizing "the talk" is essential in protecting their Black male children when confronted by police. Literature revealed "The Talk" is a term used to describe a particular type of racial socialization lesson that numerous Black parents teach their children on how to safely conduct themselves appropriately when encountering law enforcement and other individuals in positions of authority

(Anderson et al., 2022). Early education and training can foster growth among their sons, which increases their abilities to stay safe. This early education helps Black male children take on challenges, overcome setbacks, and view their efforts to build resilience and positive self-view.

Participants reported that teaching their sons about racism typically began early and often involved preparing them for rejection and discrimination and understanding that rejection and discrimination are both inevitable. Existing studies show that racial discrimination can affect the self-worth and psychological well-being of a child. The Black mothers in this study play a crucial role in the communication about race and ethnicity to their sons. The mothers shape how their sons begin to engage and interact in their communities and the whole world at large. In support of these findings, Bailey et al. (2021) shared that Black parents are more concerned with how racial discrimination might impact their children and the approaches that can be used to help them cope and thrive. The participants shared as Black mothers, it is essential to provide unconditional love and support for their sons, to raise them to be proud Black individuals, and to equip their children with the necessary knowledge relating racial discrimination and how to protect themselves when interacting with police officers.

Theme 4: Law Enforcement is Perceived as a Threat to Black Male Children

The participants perceive police officers as threats to the safety of their Black male children. These perceptions are influenced by participants' racial experiences with law enforcement or from the media showing unarmed African Americans being killed by law enforcement. In the Black community, law enforcement is viewed as heavy-handed and involves the use of excessive force in dealing with Black people, especially Black males. Participants of the current study reported that their trust in law enforcement has either decreased due to past racial experiences or they have never trusted law enforcement due to the ongoing violence against Black Americans. Following the increase in the number of police-involved killings of Black men, such as George Floyd, Daunte Wright, Tyre Nichols, and countless others, the Black community's trust in law enforcement has eroded. Nearly half of African Americans have little or no trust in police officers, as they believe that police officers treat people of color with excessive force compared to Whites (Shah, 2020). Consistently, Webb et al. (2022) suggested that Black people have been overpoliced and profiled, resulting in fatality. An interaction with the police will likely result in an outcome determined by one's skin color or unequal treatment by the judicial system. Black males have a high chance of being killed by the police in their lifespan due to the police causing over 96 deaths out of 100000 (Webb et al., 2022).

In the Black community, police officers are viewed as threats to Black male children. Although the participants appreciate the work done by police to serve and protect the people, they feel that law enforcement is part of the oppressive system that has its foundation in over-policing the Black community. The participants also feel that law enforcement was created to keep Black people enslaved, as there are some police officers who are inherently racist. The findings conform with Shah (2020), who found that 84% of Black people and 63% of Whites believe that Black people in the U.S. are treated less fairly when dealing with the police. Two of the participants who have worked with law enforcement believe that there are good police officers who are trying to make a difference, but they also acknowledge there are many incompetent police officers that have failed to protect the Black community. Police officers believe that most of the demonstrations over the killings of Black people are majorly motivated by the anti-police bias within the Black community. They believe that protestors are majorly motivated by the urge to hold police accountable. In disagreement, Zeiders et al. (2021) highlight that over 98% of the tickets given by police are to Black people who are harassed and handcuffed. Although some participants of the current study reported that only a few bad apples within the law enforcement unit make the whole department look bad, Mehra et al. (2022) disagreed by noting that over 77% of the police officers racially harass and handcuff Black people regardless of whether they cooperate or not.

Theme 5: Black Mothers Navigated the Fear of Losing Their Sons Through Educating Their Sons and Through Reliance on Faith

One of the major ways the participants overcome the fear of losing their sons through police excessive use of force is through education, awareness, and faith. Educating Black male children on how to stay safe during police encounters has become an important issue for Black mothers. Previous research confirms that, in the U.S., one of the leading causes of death for young men of color is police use of force (Edwards et al., 2019). Black males are three times more likely to be killed during police encounters compared to their White counterparts (Zeiders et al., 2021). Therefore, during police encounters, these males must stay calm, keep their hands where the police can see them, know their rights, or record when they are stopped. Complying with police demands, even if there is disrespect or violation of rights, can help Black males avoid police brutality.

Educating Black male children is an active role that the participants are willing to take to keep their sons safe from police violence. Participants reported that during police encounters, Black male children must focus on getting home safe and alive. It is important to keep their safety first. Participants also reported teaching their sons to record any interactions with police during a traffic stop. The participants also recognize that because of the nature of arbitrary, racist violence, no amount of education they provided to their sons and no amount of compliance on the part of their sons could eliminate the possibility that their sons would be killed. The participants recognize the limitations in their ability to protect their sons and the limitations in their sons' ability to protect themselves. Therefore, to cope with the fear associated with this sense of powerlessness, the participants have relied on religious faith in their fight against police brutality. In general, the church has played a pivotal role in supporting the Black community and their continued fight against racial inequality. According to Leath et al. (2020), Black churches in America have always been seen as the most independent, enduring, and influential establishments in Black communities. The fear of the possibility of losing their sons at the hands of the police and the inability to have control over the situation caused the participants to turn to their faith.

Implications of the Study

CRT draws attention to the structural ways that race is ingrained in institutional systems, such as law enforcement, reinforcing White power and increasing the likelihood that minorities (i.e., African American males and other men of color) will be treated unfairly to preserve their inferior status in positions of authority. Edwards et al. (2019) found that the use of force by law enforcement is a primary factor contributing to the mortality of young males belonging to racial and ethnic minority groups in the U.S. Black males have a far higher likelihood, almost three times greater, of being killed by police throughout their lifetime compared to their White counterparts. Recent research indicates that the occurrence of police brutality may have an adverse impact on the mental health of Black individuals (Malone Gonzalez, 2019; Roberts, 2011). Black mothers endure horrendous circumstances when law enforcement agents brutally take the lives of their sons. The senseless and brutal murders of their cherished loved ones without explanation tend to have a detrimental impact on the mental well-being of these mothers (Desmond et al., 2016). The study reveals that the Black mothers in this study suffer from fear and anxiety due to concerns about the safety of their sons, namely the risk of losing them to police brutality. These emotional challenges significantly impact their mental well-being. These Black mothers' perceptions of law enforcement were not solely shaped by their personal encounters and witnessed injustices, but these occurrences are also contextualized and linked to more extensive instances of racism and oppression. The findings of this study suggest that the participants believe that racism has a devastating effect on the process of parenting a Black male child. They assert that their sons are subjected to racist assaults that undermine their dignity, limit their prospects, and jeopardize their physical well-being. As a clinical implication, to recruit and retain Black mothers as clients, practitioners should consider employing culturally sensitive and responsive strategies. An excellent place to start would be by attempting to comprehend the historical and social context of African Americans' experiences and their connection with current incidents relating to racial violence and discrimination. It is essential for practitioners to deliberately cultivate environments that encourage open discussions, wherein Black mothers feel encouraged to share their struggles against racial oppression and resolve racial-related trauma and stress when it comes to fears of potentially losing their sons to police brutality. Therapists are encouraged to be attuned to, assess, and acknowledge the challenges faced by Black mothers both within and outside the therapeutic setting. They should also assist in developing healthy approaches for the well-being of their Black female clients. A crucial element of the therapeutic process involves providing support to Black mothers in cultivating self-love and self-acceptance while also helping them minimize the emotional energy they spend fearing the possibility of losing their sons to police violence. Here are five suggestions for therapists to use a strengths-based approach in supporting Black mothers in navigating their fear: The objectives of this treatment are to address racial and gender bias, assess for trauma, assist Black mothers in developing authenticity, aid in stress management, and examine and address manifestations of fear during therapy sessions. It is critical that Black mothers feel equipped, which can affect their mental well-being and their children's mental well-being.

Limitations

While this study provides extensive information about how Black mothers navigate their fears of potentially losing their sons during interactions with police officers, it has limitations. Given the nature of this qualitative research, a clear limitation is the limited sample size of study participants. Another limitation of this study pertains to the limited representation of Black mothers. It should be emphasized that these 10 participants do not encompass the entire population of Black mothers or their respective ethnic groups. Another limitation worth highlighting is that despite efforts to include Black mothers from various subgroups, the sample primarily consisted of educated women from high to middle socioeconomic brackets. A sample of Black mothers with diverse education and economic status may have produced different experiences. For example, considering that poor communities of color are frequently subjected to excessive policing (Alexander, 2010). Black mothers belonging to lower socioeconomic brackets may have talked about direct interactions with law enforcement and increased incidences of both community and state police violence and how this related to navigating their fear of potentially losing their sons during interactions with police officers. Finally, it is imperative to mention that Indigenous mothers and other mothers of color were excluded from this study, which does not allow for the experiences of other marginalized groups.

Recommendations for Future Research

The findings of the present study illustrate several implications for further research on the effects of law enforcement on the African American community. Further research can expand the existing knowledge about African American mothers by investigating the experiences of mothers who are raising sons in the present circumstances where exposure to police violence is a common occurrence. Studies found that Black males are at risk of getting killed by police at a much higher rate than other groups. Recent research indicates that implementing targeted policies and programs aimed at reducing violent interactions between law enforcement and African American males could potentially contribute to a decrease in deaths. The researchers suggested that efforts to lessen violent interactions between Black males and police might exist but are not being effectively publicized. In addition, developing and putting into action policies, programs, and practices aimed at lowering these kinds of violent interactions, race, and ethnicity must be taken explicitly into consideration (Calvert et al., 2020). Therefore, it is recommended that educational programs, policies, and practices are put in place for Black males to help them stay safe when encountering police officers. Given the media attention on the experiences of unarmed African American males with law enforcement, a recommendation would be to conduct research on African American father's fears of potentially losing their sons to police brutality. Given the amount of attention that has been given to African American men's interactions with law enforcement, I think it would be beneficial to find out if fathers take different approaches to navigating their fears.

Research can expand the existing knowledge of African American mothers by investigating the lived experiences of mothers raising daughters in the present circumstances, where exposure to police violence is frequent through social media. Frequently, discussions concerning violence, specifically when it pertains to the excessive use of force by the police, center on the experiences of African American adolescents and men. According to Kimberlé et al. (2023), Black women and girls have a higher likelihood of being killed by the police compared to any other group of women. Black women constitute around 10% of the female population in the U.S. However, they represent 20% of all women who are killed by the police and nearly 30% of unarmed women who are killed by the police. Including mothers and daughters in this line of research will help uncover whether they protect or educate their daughters about interactions with police officers differently than their sons.

Final recommendation: in the African American community, police are seen as a threat to Black males' safety. This means that to increase African Americans' trust in police, law enforcement agencies should do more to raise awareness about the need for better social engagement and communication with the Black community. Mentel (2012) states that the Office of Community-Oriented Policing Services was established to foster connections and develop problem-solving strategies to address crime rates and the fear of violent crimes experienced by individuals who face these challenges daily. In addition, research reported that while certain places have witnessed improvements, there has been a constant lack of progress in outcomes within Black neighborhoods. Extending future research on building trust between Black communities and law enforcement will allow an open dialogue to communicate factors contributing to mistrust and criminal activities impacting Black Americans.

Conclusion

The purpose of this qualitative phenomenological study was to explore the lived experiences, and the meaning of Black motherhood as told by Black women, recognizing how they navigate their fears of potentially losing their sons during interactions with police officers. The results of this study indicated significant negative mental, physical, and emotional effects, both for Black mothers and their male children, due to an inherently racist social system in the U.S. Participants overwhelmingly opposed the impact of racism on their children and stated that they perceived law enforcement as a threat. However, participants stated that there were positive aspects to raising a Black male child as well, notably the opportunity to pass on personal values and serve as a role model and protector for their children. Furthermore, participants stated that they were able to mitigate some of their fears of police violence through the act of educating their sons, as well as through personal faith.

References

Abrams, J. A., Hill, A., & Maxwell, M. (2019). Underneath the mask of the strong Black woman schema: Disentangling influences of strength and self-silencing on depressive symptoms among U.S. Black women. Sex Roles, 80, 517-526

Adams, C., Yin, Y., Vargas Madriz, F. L., Mullen, C. S. (2014). A phenomenology of learning large: The tutorial sphere of xMOOC video lectures. Distance Education, 35(2).

Adedoyin, A. C., Moore, S. E., Robinson, M. A., Clayton, D. M., Boamah, D. A., & Harmon, D. K. (2019). The dehumanization of Black males by police: Teaching social justice - Black life really does matter! Journal of Teaching in Social Work, 39(2), 111-131. https://doi.org/10.1080/08841233.2019.1586807

Alang, S., McAlpine, D., McCreedy, E., & Hardeman, R. (2017). Police brutality and Black health: Setting the agenda for public health scholars. American Journal of Public Health, 107(5), 662-665.

Anderson, L. A., O'Brien Caughy, M., & Owen, M. T. (2022). "The talk" and parenting while Black in America: Centering race, resistance, and refuge. Journal of Black Psychology, 48(3-4), 475–506. https://doi.org/10.1177/00957984211034294

Bailey, Z. D., Feldman, J. M., & Bassett, M. T. (2021). How structural racism works - Racist policies as a root cause of U.S. racial health inequities. New England Journal of Medicine, 384(8), 768-773.

Banaji, M. R., Fiske, S. T., & Massey, D. S. (2021). Systemic racism: Individuals and interactions, institutions, and society. Cognitive Research: Principles and Implications, 6, 1-21.

Belotto, M. J. (2018). Data analysis methods for qualitative research: Managing the challenges of coding, interrater reliability, and thematic analysis. The Qualitative Report, 23(11), 2622–2633. https://doi.org/10.46743/2160-3715/2018.3492

Blackwell, J. E. (1991). The Black community: Diversity and unity. Harper Collins Publishers

Borrell, L. N., Elhawary, J. R., Fuentes-Afflick, E., Witonsky, J., Bhakta, N., Wu, A. H., ... & Burchard, E. G. (2021). Race and genetic ancestry in medicine - A time for reckoning with racism. New England Journal of Medicine, 384(5), 474-480.

Brown, D. L. (2018). Barbaric: America's cruel history of separating children from their parents. Washington Post.

Calvert, C. M., Brady, S. S., & Jones-Webb, R. (2020). Perceptions of violent encounters between police and young Black men across stakeholder groups. Journal of Urban Health: Bulletin of the New York Academy of Medicine, 97(2), 279–295. https://doi.org/10.1007/s11524-019-00417-6

Carminati, L. (2018). Generalizability in qualitative research: A tale of two traditions. Qualitative Health Research, 28(13), 2094-2101. https://doi:10.1177/1049732318788379

Cooper, S. M., Burnett, M., Johnson, M. S., Brooks, J., Shaheed, J., & McBride, M. (2020). 'That is why we raise children': African American fathers' race-related concerns for their adolescents and parenting strategies. Journal of Adolescence, 82, 67–81. https://doi.org/10.1016/j.adolescence.2020.06.001

Cope, D. G. (2014). Methods and meanings: Credibility and trustworthiness of qualitative research. Oncology Nursing Forum, 41(1), 89–91. https://doi.org/10.1188/14.ONF.89-91

Creswell, J. W. & Poth, C. N. (2018). Qualitative inquiry & research design: Choosing among five approaches. SAGE Publications.

DeGue, S., Fowler, K. A., & Calkins, C. (2018). Deaths due to use of lethal force by law enforcement: Findings from the national violent death reporting system, 17 U.S. states, 2009-2012. American Journal of Preventive Medicine, 51(5), S173-S187.

Delgado, R., & Stefancic, J. (2020). Critical race theory: An introduction. NYU Press.

Donner, J. K., Rousseau Anderson, C., & Dixson, A. D. (2018). The more things change the more they stay the same: Race, education, and critical race theory after 20 years: An appraisal. Peabody Journal of Education, 93(1), 1-4. https://doi.org/10.1080/0161956X.2017.1403168

Doyle, L., McCabe, C., Keogh, B., Brady, A., & McCann, M. (2020). An overview of the qualitative descriptive design within nursing research. Journal of Research in Nursing, 25(5), 443–455. https://doi.org/10.1177/1744987119880234

Edwards, F., Lee, H., & Esposito, M. (2019). Risk of being killed by police use of force in the U.S. by age, race, ethnicity, and sex. Proceedings of the National Academy of Sciences, 116(34), 16793-16798.

Ekins, E. E. (2016). Policing in America: Understanding public attitudes toward the police. Results from a national survey. Results from a National Survey.

Ford, C. L., & Airhihenbuwa, C. O. (2010). Critical race theory, race equity, and public health: Toward antiracism praxis. American Journal of Public Health, 100(S1), S30-S35.

Frimpong, K. (2020). Black people are still seeking racial justice – Why and what to do about it. Brookings Institute. https://www.brookings.edu/articles/black-people-are-still-seeking-racial-justice-why-and-what-to-do-about-it/

Garcia, A. S., Taylor, S. A., & de Guzman, M. R. T. (2016). Cultural competence concepts: Contemporary racism. NebGuide. https://extensionpublications.unl.edu/assets/html/g2281/build/g2281.htm

Goble, E. & Yin, Y. (2014). Introduction to hermeneutic phenomenology: A research methodology best learned by doing it. IIQM – The Qualitative Research Blog, 16.

Hallam, J. (2004). Slavery and the making of America. PBS. https://www.thirteen.org/wnet/slavery/experience/family/history.html

Harris, D. A. (1999). Driving while Black: Racial profiling on our nation's highways. American Civil Liberties Union.

Harris, A. & Amutah-Onukagha, N. (2019). Under the radar: Strategies used by Black mothers to prepare their sons for potential police interactions. Journal of Black Psychology 45(6-7), 439-453.

Hassett-Walker, C. (2019). The racist roots of American policing: From slave patrols to traffic stops. The Conversation, 4.

Leath, S., Marchand, A. D., Harrison, A., Halawah, A., Davis, C., & Rowley, S. (2020). A qualitative exploration of Black mothers' gendered constructions of their children and their parental school involvement. Early Childhood Research Quarterly, 53, 124–135. https://doi.org/10.1016/j.ecresq.2020.03.007

Malone Gonzalez, S. (2019). Making it home: An intersectional analysis of the police talk. Gender & Society, 33(3), 363-386. https://doi.org/10.1177/0891243219828340

Marshall, C., & Rossman, G. B. (2016). Designing qualitative research. SAGE Publications.

Mays, V. M., Cochran, S. D., & Barnes, N. W. (2014). Race, race-based discrimination, and health outcomes among African Americans. Annual Review of Psychology, 58, 201-225.

Mehra, R., Alspaugh, A., Franck, L. S., McLemore, M. R., Kershaw, T. S., Ickovics, J. R., ... & Sewell, A. A. (2022). Police shootings, now that seems to be the main issue – Black pregnant women's anticipation of police brutality towards their children. BMC Public Health, 22(1), 1–8. https://doi.org/10.1186/s12889-022-12557-7

McGill, K. A. (2005). The presentation of slavery at Mount Vernon: Power, privilege, and historical truth. University of Maryland.

McLaughlin, K. (2019). Police use-of-force is a leading cause of death among young men of color, study says. Insider. https://www.insider.com/study-police-use-of-force-leading-cause-of-death-men-of-color-2019-8

Meshberg-Cohen, S., Presseau, C., Thacker, L. R., Hefner, K., & Svikis, D. (2016). Post-traumatic stress disorder, health problems, and depression among African American women in residential substance use treatment. Journal of Women's Health, 25(7), 729-737.

Moore, L. (2020). Police brutality in the U.S. Encyclopedia Britannica. https://www.britannica.com/topic/Police-Brutality-in-the-United-States-2064580.

Naderifar, M., Goli, H., & Ghaljaie, F. (2017). Snowball sampling: A purposeful method of sampling in qualitative research. Strides in Development of Medical Education, 14(3), 1-6.

Neubauer, B. E., Witkop, C. T., & Varpio, L. (2019). How phenomenology can help us learn from the experiences of others. Perspectives on Medical Education, 8, 90-97.

Omokha, R. (2021). Police violence: They were sons. Vanity Fair. https://www.vanityfair.com/news/2021/05/they-were-sons-mothers-of-black-men-killed-by-police-remember-their-losses

Ortiz, M. A. (2016). Stop resisting: An exploratory study of police brutality and its impacts on Black and Latino males, their communities, mental health, and healing.

Patton, M. Q. (2002). Qualitative research and evaluation methods. SAGE Publications.

Powell, T., & Coles, J. A. (2021). We still here: Black mothers' narratives of sense-making and resisting antiblackness and the suspensions of their Black children. Race Ethnicity and Education, 24(1), 76–95. https://doi.org/10.1080/13613324.2020.1718076

Richardson Jr., J. B., Van Brakle, M., & St. Vil, C. (2014). Taking boys out of the hood. Exile as a parenting strategy for African American male youth. New Directions for Child and Adolescent Development, 2014(143), 11-31.

Riley, J. R. (2011). Racism, discrimination, and prejudice: Through the voices of undergraduate black men at predominately white institutions. Doctoral dissertation, University of Georgia.

Rogers, A. (2015). How police brutality harms mothers: Linking police violence to the reproductive justice movement. Hastings Race & Poverty, 12, 205.

Scott, C. L. (2007). A discussion of individual, institutional, and cultural racism, with implications for HRD. Online Submission.

Shah, K. (2020). Mothers of Black Americans killed by police speak out: 'nothing's changed.' The Guardian. https://www.theguardian.com/us-news/2020/jun/11/mothers-black-children-killed-by-police-speak-out

Smith Lee, J. R., & Robinson, M. A. (2019). That's my number one fear in life. It's the Police: Examining young Black men's exposures to trauma and loss resulting from police violence. Journal of Black Psychology, 45(3), 143-184.

Solomon, D., Maxwell, C., & Castro, A. (2019). Systematic inequality and American democracy. Center for American Progress. https://www.americanprogress.org/issues/race/reports/2019/08/07/473003/systematicinequality-american-democracy.

Thompson, C. L. (2021). Fatal police shootings of unarmed Black people reveal troubling patterns. NPR. https://www.npr.org/2021/01/25/956177021/fatal-police-shootings-of-unarmed-black-people-reveal-troubling-patterns

Turner, J. L. (2020). Black mothering in action: The racial-class socialization practices of low-income Black single mothers. Sociology of Race and Ethnicity, 6(2), 242-253. https://doi.org/10.1177/2332649219899683

Webb, L., Jackson, D. B., Jindal, M., Alang, S., Mendelson, T., & Clary, L. K. (2022). Anticipation of racially motivated police brutality and youth mental health. Journal of Criminal Justice, p. 83, 101967. https://doi.org/10.1016/j.jcrimjus.2022.101967

West, E. (2019). The double-edged sword of motherhood under American slavery. Uncommon Sense – The Blog.

Williams, D. R. (2018). Stress and the mental health of populations of color: Advancing our understanding of race-related stressors. Journal of Health and Social Behavior, 59(4), 466-485.

Williams, D. R. & Rucker, T. D. (2000). Understanding and addressing racial disparities in health care. Health Care Financing Review, 21(4), 75.

Williams, H. A. (2021). How slavery affected African American families. Slavery and the making of America. PBS. https://www.thirteen.org/wnet/slavery/experience/family/history.html

Williams, J. H. (2018). Child separations and families divided: America's history of separating children from their parents. Social Work Research, 42(3), 141–146.

Wood, K. E. (2012). Gender and sexuality, slavery, and abolition of slavery. In M. M. Smith & R. L. Paquette (Eds.), The Oxford handbook of slavery in the Americas. Oxford University Press.

Yin, R. K. (2018). Case study research and applications: Design and methods. Sage.

Zeiders, K. H., Umaña-Taylor, A. J., Carbajal, S., & Pech, A. (2021). Police discrimination among Black, Latina/x/o, and White adolescents: Examining frequency and relations to academic functioning. Journal of Adolescence, 90, 91-99. https://doi.org/10.1016/j.adolescence.2021.06.001

APPENDIX A

Email to Participants

Email to Participants

The invitation email subject line will be: Invitation Email looking for Black mothers interested in being a participant in a research study. The email content will say: Thank you for your interest in this study. My name is Michelle Wright. I am a Couple and Family PsyD student at Alliant International University. I am conducting a qualitative research study as a partial requirement for my Doctoral degree in Psychology. Dr. Tatiana Glebova, Ph.D., LMFT Professor of Alliant International University/CSPP/Couple & Family Therapy Program, is my chair and will be the supervisor throughout this study. The research is entitled "Black Mothers in The U.S. Fear their Sons' Death by Racism." It will explore how Black mothers navigate their fears of potentially losing their sons during interactions with police officers. I am specifically seeking participants who identify as Black mothers with at least one Black son. If you are interested in this study, I will email a consent form for an overview. At the agreed interview location, you can ask questions before signing the consent form either in person or, if you prefer, virtually through Zoom; you may sign electronically. You will be asked to do a one-on-one interview with me, which may last up to 1 ½ -2 hours. Appreciating your time and support, you will receive a $20.00 visa gift card or a $20.00 donation to a charity of your choice. Light refreshments will be provided during the interview. For more information on being a volunteer participant, please kindly respond to this email at mwright1@alliant.edu or call (916) 538-8060 or contact Dr. Tatiana Glebova at tglebova@alliant.edu or call (916) 561-3214. Thank you for your consideration.

Sincerely,
Michelle Wright AMFT
Alliant International University.

APPENDIX B

Informed Consent Agreement

Informed Consent Agreement

You are invited to participate in a research study. Please read this consent form so that you understand what your participation will involve. Before you consent to participate, please ask any questions to be sure you understand what your participation will involve.

Institutional Contact:
Alliant International University
Couple and Family PsyD
2030 W. EL Camino Ave
Sacramento, CA 95833
(916) 750-2235

Introduction:
My name is Michelle Wright. I am an Alliant International University student pursuing a Doctor of Psychology degree in Couple & Family Therapy. I am inviting you to take part in a research study. Before you decide to participate in this study, it is essential that you understand why the research is being done and what it will involve. You should be aware that you can withdraw from this study at any time. Please read the following information below carefully.

The topic of Study:
"Black Mothers in The U.S. Fear their Sons' Death by Racism."

Purpose of Study:
This qualitative study aims to explore the lived experiences and the meaning of Black motherhood as told by Black women, recognizing how they navigate their fears of potentially losing their sons during interactions with police officers. Every year Black families lose children

to police killings. A population is being overlooked in the wake of these unexpected killings: Black mothers. As the researcher, I believe that you can help by telling your story. Your participation in this research will help Black mothers understand and navigate their fears surrounding the possibility of losing their sons to police violence. You will be selected as a possible participant in this study because it is essential that your voice be heard.

Procedures:
This research will involve your participation in a phenomenological qualitative study. Methods will include a demographic questionnaire, face-to-face audio-recorded interview, and field notes. The interview will take one and a half to two hours to complete. After you sign the consent form, you and I will agree upon a day, time, and location for the interview. The location will include a reserved room at a local library of our choice. The interviewer will reserve the room a week in advance and observe the space before conducting the interview to ensure we have a private, quiet room. For your comfort, you can do the interview virtually through Zoom, which will be video-recorded and held in the reserve library room. No one else but the interviewer will be present. As a participant, you will complete a demographic questionnaire prior to recorded interviews, providing data on your age, gender, racial/ethnic identity, number and gender of your children, relational status, the highest level of education, employment, and income. No other personal information, such as your name or address, will be collected. The recorded information is confidential, and no one else except Dr. Tatiana Glebova, Chair Supervisor, will access the information documented during your interview. After each interview, the recordings will be stored on a password-protected thumb drive. A second copy of the recordings will be held on a password-protected thumb drive in a secure secondary location as a backup if the primary copy is destroyed. The researcher will retain information, audio records, transcripts, or notes for (5) years after completing the research and will then be destroyed using a Shred-it system. The researcher will happily share the cumulative findings with you after completing

completing the research study.

Risks:
Potential risks are that participants may experience unpleasant emotions such as anxiety, sadness, anger, and difficulty regulating emotions as a result of participating in this study. To minimize any risks you might experience, the researcher will closely monitor your mental and emotional status throughout the face-to-face interviews. The researcher will check-in with you at the end of the interview if needed to offer a follow-up phone call. As a participant, you do not have to answer any questions or give any reason for not responding to the questions in the interview if you wish. After completing the consent form, you will be provided with counseling referrals and emergency contacts should you need them due to the impact of the topic being discussed. The responsibility of any occurring cost for the counseling referrals will be the participant's responsibility, and the emergency contact will be a free service.

Benefits of Participation:
As a researcher, I hope as a participant; your voice will be utilized for justice for your sons and other victims of police brutality and you will provide valuable information that will capture the attention of law enforcement, lawmakers, marriage and family therapists, other clinicians, and those in a position to end the persistent inequalities and injustice of African American males. However, there may be no personal benefits of participation for you.

Incentives for/costs to participation:
In appreciation of your time and support, after the interview, you will receive a $20.00 visa gift card in-person or if the interview is conducted via Zoom you will receive a $20.00 visa eGift card through your email (The researcher buys the card online load money the participant receives the eGift card via email). Due to the length of the interview, you may have light refreshment during the interview.

Confidentiality:
The records from this study will be kept as confidential as possible. No individual identifying information (e.g., real names) will be used in any reports or publications resulting from this study. All methods will be given codes instead of your name and stored on a password-protected thumb drive in the personal possession of the researcher. Research information will be kept in a locked, secure file. Only the researcher and chair supervisor will have access to the files. Participant data will be kept confidential except in cases where the researcher, as a mandated reporter, is legally obligated to report specific incidents. These incidents include, but may not be limited to, known or suspected abuse or neglect relating to children, elders, or dependent adults. Abuse can include physical, sexual, or emotional abuse. Suicide risk will consist of harm to self or injury to others.

Counseling Resources/Help Line

Alliance Family Counseling Services
(310) 919-4252 (Sliding Scale and All PPO insurance)
Certified and trained in various treatment interventions such as grief and loss, depression, anxiety, trauma, self-injury, and disruptive behavioral disorders, including ADHD.

Sacramento County Mental Health
(916) 875-1055 (Medi-Cal insurance and Sliding Scale)
Therapeutic services focused on issues impacting the Black and African American communities.

Hope for Healthy Families Counseling Center
(916) 686-9209 (Sliding Scale starting at $40.00 a session)
Work with a wide range of emotional and behavioral issues providing services that span from therapy for depression and grief counseling to parenting support, couples counseling, and beyond.

Aldea Counseling Services (ACS)
(707) 425-9670 (Sliding Scale most insurances)
ACS empowers people to improve their mental health and family functioning, creating a safer and healthier community. The program encompasses a wide range of mental health services.
The NAMI HelpLine: Call 1-800-950-NAMI (6264), text "HelpLine" to 62640, or email us at helpline@nami.org
National Suicide Prevention Lifeline 1-800-273-8255
For general questions about the rights of research, participants contact the Alliant International University Institutional Review Board at Alliant-irb@alliant.edu
Researcher & Supervisor Contact:
Principal Investigator:

Michelle Wright AMFT,
Alliant International University
(916) 583-0860
Mwright1@alliant.edu

Chair Supervisor:
Alliant International University
Tatiana Glebova Ph.D., LMFT
Professor, Alliant International University/CSPP/Couple & Family Therapy Program, Sacramento, Ca
 (916) 561-3214
Tglebova@alliant.edu
In order to ensure that you have access to the phone numbers and emails of contact persons responsible for the oversight, supervision, or completion of this study, please either download or print this consent form before proceeding with this study.
Before signing this consent form, please talk to the researcher to clarify anything on this consent form or any concerns you have about participating in this research study.

Signature:

I have read the previous information, or it has been read to me. I have had the opportunity to ask questions, which have been answered to my satisfaction. I consent voluntarily to be a participant in this study.

Print Name of Participant_____
Signature of Participant _____
Date _____

I confirm that the participant was given an opportunity to ask questions about the study. All the questions asked by the participants were answered correctly and to the best of my ability. I confirm that the individual has not been coerced into giving consent, and the consent has been given freely and voluntarily.

Print Name of Researcher/person taking the consent_____
Signature of Researcher /person taking the consent_____
Date _____

APPENDIX C

Demographic Information

Demographic Information

Age:
Ethnicity: (circle answer)
African- American
Black
Black-American
Afro-American
From multiple races (but Identify as Black)
Some other race (Please be Specify)

What is your Parental Status? (circle answer)

Biological mother   Stepmother   Adoptive mother

Do you have children? (circle)   Yes   No

What number of sons are you parenting or live outside the household? (add number below)

Relational Status: (circle answer)
Married
Divorced
Separated
Widowed
Never Married

Education: (circle answer)
What is the highest level of school you have completed or highest degree you have received?
Less than a high school degree
Highschool degree or equivalent (e.g., GED)
Some college but no degree
Associate degree
Bachelor degree
Graduate degree
Ph.D. degree

Employment:
What is your profession?   Retired   Disable Not Working   (add profession below or circle answer)

Household Income: (circle answer)
$0 - $9,999
$10,000 - $19,999
$20,000 - $29,999
$30,000 - $39,999
$40,000 - $49,999
$50,000 - $59,999
$60,000 - $69,999
$70,000 - $79,999
$80,000 - $89,999
$90,000 - $99,999
$100,000 - more

APPENDIX D

Interview Questions

Interview Questions

How do Black mothers navigate their fears of potentially losing their sons during interactions with police officers?

Question 1: Motherhood:
1) How would you describe motherhood as a Black woman?
2) What are the benefits of raising a Black male child?
3) What are the challenges in raising a Black male child?
4) What do you think makes raising a Black son different than raising boys of a different race?
5) What are your strengths and resiliency as a Black mother raising a Black male child in a racist society?
6) What might you tell future mothers of Black sons?

Question 2: Experiences of Racism:

1) Have you experienced racism in your life, if so, what would be some examples?
2) How might racism impact your role as a mother?
3) Have you tried to educate your son about racism, if so, when did you start educating him/them and what message (s) did you tell them?
4) How have you attempted to protect your son against racism?
5) How have your son (s) experiences with racism influenced them?
6) How has racism impacted your health, relationships, and lived experience as a Black woman?

Question 3: Police Interactions:

1) What are your views about police officers overall in today's society?
2) Do you believe police officers treat Black boys and Black men differently than other ethnicities? How so?
3) Have you ever experienced racial discrimination at the hands of a police officer?
4) Have you tried to educate your son (s) about interactions with police officers?
5) Did you see any stories about police brutality on television, media, or print, if so, how did witnessing these stories impact you as a mother?
6) If you could talk to a police captain, officer, or lawmakers what might you tell them?

APPENDIX E

Recruitment Flyer

Recruitment Flyer

Dissertation Title:
"Black Mothers in The United States Fear their Sons' Death by Racism"

RESEARCH PARTICIPANTS NEEDED FOR INTERVIEW

Wanted:
African American Black Mothers with at least one or more Black sons.
Interview: Expected Completion Time Approximately 1.5-2 Hours

Criteria
Identify as Black Female
Potential Participants must be biological, step, or adoptive mothers:
18 + Years Old
English Speaker
U.S. Resident

Please contact:
Michelle Wright, Principle Investigator, with any questions at
mwright1@alliant.edu
or (916) 538-8060

The Purpose of the Study: This qualitative phenomenological study explores the lived experiences and the meaning of Black motherhood as told by Black women, aiming to understand how they navigate their fears of potentially losing their sons during interactions with police officers. Every year Black families lose children to police killings. A population is being overlooked in the wake of these unexpected killings: Black Mothers. As the researcher, I believe that you can help by telling your story. Your participation in this research will help Black mothers understand and navigate their fears surrounding the possibility of losing their sons to police violence; it is critical to provide support in allowing Black women to utilize and maximize their voice in this experience.

Approved by Alliant International University Institutional Review Board

Author Bio

Dr. Michelle R. Wright-Carter was born and raised in Vallejo, CA. She is a wife, mother, and grandmother. She attended Alliant International University, where she received a Doctor of Psychology degree in Marriage and Family Therapy, California State University Sacramento with a master's degree in Marriage and Family Therapy, and the University of California Davis with an undergraduate degree in Sociology. She has over two decades of experience in the Mental Health field. She is fully committed and determined to work with and advocate for individuals facing setbacks to help them manage their illnesses, overcome challenges, and lead productive lives. If given the proper guidance, she believes every client can find a path to their own personal success. African American women writers have helped bring the Black woman's experience to life for millions of readers, and she is honored to be a part of that experience. Dr. Michelle Wright-Carter is the author of "Every Step a Prayer: The Lives of Black Mothers Raising Black Sons." She answered the call to write on the subject of the lives of Black mothers raising their sons in a racist society and is thrilled to share that book with you.

www.ingramcontent.com/pod-product-compliance
Lightning Source LLC
Chambersburg PA
CBHW052032030426
42337CB00027B/4963